Thomas Hardy

Stories in Black and White

Thomas Hardy

Stories in Black and White

ISBN/EAN: 9783337005153

Printed in Europe, USA, Canada, Australia, Japan

Cover: Foto ©Thomas Meinert / pixelio.de

More available books at **www.hansebooks.com**

STORIES IN
BLACK AND WHITE

BY

THOMAS HARDY   J. M. BARRIE
W. E. NORRIS   W. CLARK RUSSELL
Mrs. OLIPHANT   Mrs. E. LYNN LINTON
GRANT ALLEN   JAMES PAYN

WITH TWENTY-SEVEN ILLUSTRATIONS

NEW YORK
D. APPLETON AND COMPANY
1893

CONTENTS.

LIST OF ILLUSTRATIONS.

THE ROMANCE OF MADAME DE CHANTELOUP.

By W. E. NORRIS.

I.

W. E. NORRIS.

WELL, after all, I don't know that there was anything so very romantic about the poor woman's story ; not much more, at least, than there is in a score of other stories which have come to the knowledge of an old fellow who has lived, and still to some extent lives, in the world, who has kept his eyes and ears open, who is a bachelor, and who, for some reason or other, has been honoured by the confidence of numerous fortunate and unfortunate persons. When I come to think of it, I am constrained to admit, somewhat unwillingly, that the ensuing narrative is redeemed from being absolutely commonplace chiefly, if not solely, by the circumstance that Madame de Chanteloup's name—so long as it is remembered at all—will be remembered in connection with that of a reigning monarch. It was not on that account that I personally felt interested in her. In the course of a wandering existence it has been my lot to be brought into contact with many Royalties, and it is a long time since their presence ceased to inspire me with that thrill of awe and admiration which they are able to convey to the great majority of such among their fellow-beings as do not hate them on principle. In the city which for upwards of twenty years has been my home it is customary to affirm that *Les rois s'en vont.* I do not know whether this is true or not; but if it be the case that the form of government which they represent is in a fair way towards being discarded by civilized nations, I really do believe that they will owe their downfall not so much to any sins of their own, or of those who act under them, as to their striking lack of individuality.

Now, that is a defect which nobody could think of imputing to Madame de Chanteloup. Other shortcomings were, truly or falsely, laid to her charge; but after the affair of early youth which brought her into notoriety, and to which I shall have occasion to refer more particularly by-and-by, all who enjoyed the privilege of her acquaintance were compelled to admit that she was not *la première venue.* Her hastily-arranged marriage with that broken-down scamp the Comte de Chanteloup did not prove a happy one—considering what the cir-

cumstances and what his character and habits
were, it could not possibly have turned out otherwise than as it did—but she managed to make
herself respected, she managed to rise above reach
of the faintest breath of scandal (even Chanteloup himself, when in a melting mood after
dinner, used to describe her, with tears in his
eyes, as an angel in the disguise of a beautiful
woman), and she accomplished a still more
difficult feat than that, inasmuch as she contrived to render her modest abode in the Fau-
bourg Saint-Germain one of the most exclusive
of Parisian houses.   When her husband rid
society of a singularly useless and disreputable
member by breaking his neck over a fence at
Vincennes, she preferred residing all by herself
in the land of her adoption to returning to her
friends and relatives in England.   Perhaps she
had not a large number of friends or relatives
left; perhaps, if she had, they did not solicit
her company as warmly as they might have

done. Upon those points I cannot speak with certainty; but, having been honoured by admission into the small circle of her Parisian intimates, I can say that we should have been inconsolable had she thought fit to leave us.

After a decent period of mourning, she began to entertain in a quiet way. Her dinners, though unpretending, were irreproachably served; the guests who gathered round her table were almost always notable from one cause or another, and it was seldom that there was not amongst them at least one who wore a scarlet, a violet, or a black cassock. She was excessively and rigidly pious—more so, perhaps, in her actions than in her words; although it was very well understood that the free style of conversation which has become so fashionable in the last years of this century must not be indulged in under her roof. To tell the truth, I think we were all a little bit afraid of her. It sounds rather absurd, no doubt, for a man of my years to talk about being afraid of a woman who might very well have been his grand-daughter; but many people must have good reason to be aware that we do not, as a rule, grow braver as we grow older, and Madame de Chanteloup, with her tall figure, her clearly-cut features, her blue eyes, and a certain air of austerity which she knew very well how to assume, really was not a person with whom it would have been safe to take a liberty of any sort or kind. The mere fact of her youth had nothing to say to the matter.

Other juveniles, however, are considerably less formidable, and I certainly felt that my grey hairs gave me a right to say anything that I might deem fitting to young Eyre Pome-roy when he looked me up, one morning, at my modest quarters in the Rue Tronchet just as I was finishing my mid-day breakfast.

"Look here, Mr. Wortley," began this young gentleman, whose well-proportioned frame, closely-cut black hair and grey eyes would have entitled him to be called handsome even if he had not possessed in other respects the traditional beauty of his race, "I want you to tell me something. I want you to tell me what you know of the Comtesse de Chanteloup's history."

"Oh, is that all?" said I, handing him a cigarette. "Well, I know a good many things about a good many ladies which I don't quite see my way to imparting to an over-grown school-boy like you. Why should I gratify your curiosity with regard to bygone episodes, which Madame de Chanteloup probably would not wish me to allude to, in the presence of those who happen to be ignorant of them?"

"Only because I am going to marry her, I hope, and because she referred me to you," answered my young friend composedly.

"The deuce you are!—and the deuce she did!" I exclaimed; for I was not a little taken aback by an announcement, which was scarcely less astonishing to me than it would have been to hear that Mr. Pomeroy was about to espouse the Empress Dowager of China. " Mercy upon us! What can have persuaded either you or her to behave in such an unnatural way? I thought you were barely acquainted with her."

He explained that he was better acquainted with her than I imagined, that he had fallen in love with her at first sight (which, if surprising, was at all events not inconceivable), that he had seen her pretty constantly during the few weeks which he had spent in Paris, that he had ended by making her an offer of his hand and heart, and that she had not refused him.

" She did," he added, by way of an after-thought, " make it a *sine quâ non* that I should join the Church of Rome—feeling so strongly as she does upon those subjects, one can't wonder at her having insisted upon that—but I told her I had no objection."

" Oh, indeed!" said I. " That, I suppose,

was a concession too trifling to be worth dis-
puting about. And you live in Donegal, and
your father is a prominent Orangeman. Afterwards ? "

" Oh, well, if you come to that," returned
Mr. Pomeroy, " we're a branch of the Catholic
Church—at least, I've always understood that
we claimed to be—and, as she says, the whole
question narrows itself to one of acknowledging
the supreme authority of the Pope—— "

" Your father," I interrupted, " doubtless
joins once a year, with religious fervour, in
the Orange battle-cry of 'To Hell with the
Pope !' "

" I don't believe he does anything so dis-
graceful and uncharitable ; and I dare say the
Pope is all right—why shouldn't he be ? Well,
then, afterwards ? Afterwards she told me
that there were events connected with her past
life which might make it impossible for her to
marry me, and that I had better go and ask you

2

what they were. She said you were the sort of old chap who knew all about other people's business."

Of course I was perfectly well aware that Madame de Chanteloup was incapable of having described me in such false and vulgar terms; still it did seem probable that she had wished to cast upon me a task which she had found too painful to undertake on her own account, and the question was whether I was in any way bound to oblige her. Was I to rake up the cinders of a burnt-out scandal for the benefit of this ridiculous youth, who had brought an introduction to me from his father a few weeks before, and who would most undoubtedly be forbidden by his family to contract any such alliance as that upon which he had set his callow affections? Was I to relate how in years gone by there had been—what shall I call it?—a rather pronounced flirtation between Madame de Chanteloup, then a mere slip of

a girl, and the heir-apparent to a certain
throne; how there had been a tremendous row
about it; how that unconscionable old mother
of hers, Mrs. Wilbraham, had threatened to
make revelations which could not possibly be
permitted; and how, finally, the Comte de
Chanteloup had been induced to marry her
by the payment of his debts and a large sum
of ready money? All things considered, I
really did not conceive it to be my duty to
do this, and I confined myself to vague references to current rumours, which my young
gentleman indignantly scouted.

"What vile lies!" he cried. "I'm glad you
don't state them as truths; but if any man ever
dares to say they are true before me—well, I'll
promise him a bad quarter of an hour. How
can she have supposed that I should ever waste
a second thought upon the calumnies of reptiles,
who most likely have never seen her in their
lives? Why, no man with eyes in his head

could look at her and doubt that she was as innocent as an infant."

I shrugged my shoulders and held my tongue. I am old, and even when I was young I had no taste for unnecessary quarrels. Besides, what is the use of arguing with a man who is in love? It was as certain as anything could be that Pomeroy's father would never permit him to marry a Papist with a dubious record; and, that being so, I naturally paid little heed to the rhapsodies with which the boy proceeded to favour me. I had heard that kind of thing so many, many times before! What was really interesting and inexplicable was Madame de Chanteloup's conduct in the matter, and I will not deny that I went that evening to a party at which I thought it likely that she might be present for the express purpose of observing her and giving her a chance to enlighten me.

I can't say whether or not she attended that

"WELL," SAID SHE; "AND OF COURSE YOU TOLD HIM—ALL THAT THERE
WAS TO BE TOLD."

party for the express purpose of meeting the reader's humble servant; but she behaved very much as though that had been her motive, for no sooner had I shaken hands with my hostess than she sailed straight across the room towards me and beckoned me aside, with a certain imperious air which was habitual to her. She was always pale; but I fancied that she looked rather whiter than usual that evening; so I opened the conversation by saying: "I am afraid you have one of your neuralgic headaches."

"Yes," she answered; "I am in great pain, and I have been in great pain all day. That is one reason why I could not see your friend Mr. Pomeroy when he called. He was with you this morning, I presume?"

I answered that he had been with me, and looked politely interrogative.

"Well," said she; "and of course you told him—all that there was to be told."

"I am not sure that it was in my power to do that," replied I. "I told him of certain rumours which, as you are aware, are *le secret de Polichinelle*, and I should not have informed him of them if I had not gathered that you wished me to do so."

"Of course I wished you to do so. And what did he say?"

"Oh, he simply snapped his fingers at them. He attached no more importance to calumny than he did to such a trifle as changing his religion at your behest."

A faint tinge of colour came into her cheeks and the slightly severe expression of her face relaxed for a moment. She resumed it, however, in order to remark:

"You are a sceptic" (this was quite untrue, but no matter); "you believe a great deal more in politics than you do in religion, and I should never be able to persuade you that a man who adopts the only true faith is not what you would call a turncoat. Perhaps it may have been my good fortune to do Mr. Pomeroy one very real service, although it may be impossible for me to grant him all he asks me for."

"Can you really be contemplating such an unscrupulous trick as that?" I exclaimed; "and can you imagine that it has the remotest chance of success?"

She did not deign to answer; but indeed I required no answer. Her face told me plainly enough that she was actually in love with that impetuous youth, and that she wished, if she could, to accept him. I fancied also that she was not less grateful to me than he had been for merely mentioning as reports what I might almost have ventured, but for my cautious disposition, to affirm as ascertained facts. She dismissed me presently with a friendly little motion of her head, and turned to speak to one of the men who had been hovering near her during our short colloquy. I don't mind acknowledging that I should have been glad if she had been a little more communicative; still I was not altogether sorry that she had refrained from honouring me by asking my advice; for, had she seen fit to do so, I could not, in common honesty and charity, have counselled her to do otherwise than refuse a suitor whom it would have been wiser to refuse in the first instance. She was one of the best and one of the most charming women in the world; but—well, the "buts" appeared to me to be of overwhelming cogency.

Why had she not adopted that easy and obvious plan? Nobody possessing the most elementary acquaintance with her sex would attempt to answer such a question; but, as regards this particular case, I have a theory, which may or may not be correct. I think Madame de Chanteloup was a curiously con- scientious woman; I think she would not, under any circumstances, have consented to tell

"I WAS STROLLING DOWN THE CHAMPS ELYSÉES ONE AFTERNOON, . . . WHEN
A PAIR OF EQUESTRIANS CANTERED PAST ME, IN WHOM I RECOGNIZED THE
FAIR COUNTESS AND HER IMPOSSIBLE ADORER."

a lie; and I suspect that when young Pomeroy asked her point-blank whether she loved him or not, she felt unable to reply in the negative. Being thus situated, she had (or, at least, so I imagined) imposed a couple of trying tests upon him, half hoping, half fearing that they would prove a little too severe for him to face.

Be that as it may, I neither saw nor heard any more of her or of him for a full week. At the expiration of that time I was strolling down the Champs Elysées one afternoon, on my way back from the Bois de Boulogne, where I had been breakfasting with a few friends, when a pair of equestrians cantered past me, in whom I recognized the fair Countess and her impossible adorer. I was sorry to see them together; for, although I knew that Madame de Chanteloup was in the habit of riding every day, and that their meeting might have been purely accidental, I could not but be aware that she would never have allowed the young fellow to join her if she had not contemplated granting him greater privileges than that; and really, for her own sake, it would have been so very much better to grant him no privileges at all.

That my forebodings were only too well founded was proved to me long ere I reached the Place de la Concorde. Young Pomeroy came galloping back, jumped off his horse, and, gripping me by the arm, said—

"Congratulate me, Mr. Wortley! I know you're a true friend of hers, as well as of mine, and I'm sure you'll be glad to hear that it's all right."

"Do you mean," I inquired, "that you have obtained your father's consent to your marriage?"

"My father's consent?—good gracious me, no! As if I had had any excuse to ask him for it! But I have obtained hers, which is a good deal more to the purpose. She says she's willing to trust me if I am willing to trust her; she says that if I will consent to be received into her Church, and if I will never allude again to that—that infernal blasphemy (for I really can't call it by any other name) which you mentioned to me the other day—— "

" And which, of course, you are prepared to treat with the contempt that it deserves," I interjected.

" My dear sir, am I a born fool ? "

I thought it extremely probable that he was; but I was too polite to say so, and he went on—

" Is it likely that, knowing her as I do, I should believe there was even the remotest possibility of her ever having done anything of which she ought to be ashamed ? Is it likely that I should wish to insult her by prying into bygones which she would rather not talk about ? Do you suppose I should enjoy relating to her the whole history of my own past

life ?   And what business have I to refuse her
an indulgence which I claim for myself?"

He proceeded to point out, at great length,
and in glowing language, how infinitely higher,
nobler, and purer Madame de Chanteloup must
needs be than himself.   I was not concerned to
contradict him ; I do not assert, and never
have asserted, that the world's estimate of what
is pardonable in a man and unpardonable in a
woman is intrinsically just ; only, as we live in
the world, we must take it as we find it ; and
I confess that I was a little disappointed in
Madame de Chanteloup, who, I thought, might
have spared this youthful enthusiast the inevitable shock which awaited him.

However, as I said before, nobody who
understands women, however imperfectly, attempts to account for their conduct, and I own
that my heart became softened towards the
woman who is the subject of this sketch when
I met her, the next day, at the entrance of the

church of St. Germain l'Auxerrois, where, I
suppose, she had been saying her prayers. I
was tolerably well acquainted with her features,
for which, indeed, I had always had a very
sincere and profound admiration; but at that
moment they wore an expression which was
wholly unfamiliar to me, and which somehow
made her look like what I imagined she must
have looked like as a child. The poor woman
was happy, in fact; Heaven knows that her
life had not hitherto been favoured with any
too large a share of happiness!

I don't remember what I said to her—something congratulatory and commonplace, no
doubt—but it did not matter what I said, for
she evidently was not listening to me. Only,
as I was helping her into her brougham, she
grasped my hand with unusual warmth, and
exclaimed, " Ah, Mr. Wortley, the world is not
so bad as we try to make it out. There are
noble and generous hearts even among men."

I was not aware of having ever maintained the contrary; but I was sorely afraid that she would be driven into doing so before long; for Eyre Pomeroy, however noble and generous he might be, was dependent upon his father, and it was hardly in the nature of things that his father's nobility and generosity should display themselves in the especial form of which she appeared to be thinking. Still, if my fullest sympathy and my best wishes could have done her any good, they would have been as much at her service as I myself was. Unhappily, neither I nor my sympathy could obliterate an episode of which every proof and detail was easily procurable.

II.

I NEED scarcely say that the news of the Comtesse de Chanteloup's betrothal to her young compatriot, and of the latter's impend-

ing admission into the bosom of the Holy
Roman Church, was very soon bruited abroad ;
nor is it necessary for me to add that this
unexpected piece of intelligence set many
tongues in motion. I suppose Pomeroy told
everybody ; probably the Countess herself was
too proud to keep silence ; anyhow, all Paris
was placed in possession of the fact, and very
sorry I was that all Paris should thus be
entitled to make observations which, had they
been reported to the persons chiefly concerned,
could hardly have failed to cause them pain.
For my own part, I am not ashamed to ac-
knowledge that I hoped the boy would stand to
his guns, seeing that, if the worst came to the
worst, and his family cast him adrift, his wife's
fortune would suffice to keep him and her out
of want. He was only a boy, after all, and no
doubt, if I had been his father, I should have
done my utmost to restrain him from rashly
compromising his whole future career ; but I

was not his father; I was both powerless and irresponsible, and I could not for the life of me help inwardly espousing the cause of poor Madame de Chanteloup.

One afternoon an event for which I had been fully prepared took place. My servant brought me a card, which bore the name of Sir Francis Pomeroy, and announced that the gentleman was waiting to hear whether I would receive him. Of course I had to send out a request that he would do me the honour to come in. I did not know much about him; I had met him perhaps half a dozen times in years gone by. I was intimate with some of his relations, and I had written a polite reply to the letter of introduction which had been delivered to me by his son. It seemed probable that he had now come to upbraid me for having led his son into a *guet-apens*. However, the tall, spare, grey-headed gentleman who was presently ushered into my presence proved as reasonable in behaviour as he was courteous in manner.

" I have taken the liberty of calling upon you before letting Eyre know of my arrival, Mr. Wortley," he began, " because it will make an unpleasant task somewhat easier for me if I can obtain beforehand from a disinterested source some account of this unfortunate entanglement of his. You will allow that it is an unfortunate entanglement ? "

" I don't know that I should describe it as an entanglement," I replied. " I suppose I must call it unfortunate by reason of certain rumours which are tolerably notorious, and which may even have reached your ears."

" They have not only reached my ears," said Sir Francis, composedly, " but I have taken pains to verify them. I have been at our Embassy to-day, and also at the —— Lega-tion " (for obvious reasons I suppress the nationality of the Legation that he mentioned),

3

" and the result is that I have been allowed to
see documents which place the affair altogether
out of the category of rumours.   There it all
is in black and white—the private or semi-
private instructions of the Prince's Government, the pressure brought to bear by our own
people, the Comte de Chanteloup's demands,
and his formal acknowledgment of the receipt
of a sum of money for a specific purpose.   I
was not, it is true, allowed to take copies of
these papers, and I was warned that they
could never be made public ; but, of course, nothing of that kind is necessary for my purpose.
What I have seen amply justifies me in saying
that I cannot permit my son to marry a woman
with such a record as Madame de Chanteloup's.
I won't speak of his proposed change of religion.
It is a subject upon which I feel strongly ; but
the point really doesn't arise, and need not
be alluded to.   My only wish is not to make
myself more disagreeable to Eyre than I can

help; so I should be glad if you wouldn't mind telling me whether he is ignorant of the circumstances, and whether, in that event, you had any good reason for keeping him in ignorance of them."

This was a little awkward, but I made out as good a case as I could for myself, and I tried also—though I knew it would be useless—to make out as good a case as I could for Madame de Chanteloup. Sir Francis listened to me with perfect politeness and good temper; he even expressed sympathy with the unfortunate lady, who, he said, might very likely have been more sinned against than sinning.

" Only, of course," he added, " it's out of the question for my son to marry her."

" You mean," I could not help observing, " that you will forbid him to marry her. Isn't it possible, though, that he may insist upon marrying her, notwithstanding your prohibition ? "

" Such a thing is possible, but I cannot think it at all likely. You see, Mr. Wortley, both you and Madame de Chanteloup have—well, I won't say you have deceived him; but at all events you haven't enlightened him. It devolves upon me to do that, and, painful though the duty is, I should be inexcusable if I evaded it."

I could not urge him to refrain from doing what any father would have done in his place; but I did venture to remind him that he was not quite entitled to speak of Madame de Chanteloup as a woman of damaged reputation. " When all is said," I remarked, " there remains a doubt, and I think she might be allowed the benefit of it."

" I have no wish to be uncharitable," answered Sir Francis, getting up; " but what there cannot be the slightest doubt about is that the Comte de Chanteloup was paid to marry this lady, that the money was provided by the

father of the present king, and that Mrs. Wilbraham threatened to make damaging disclosures if
the required sum was not forthcoming. From
those undisputed facts most people would say
that only one conclusion could be drawn."

I was not under any illusion as to what most
people would say, and in fact did say, about
this melancholy business ; yet I felt pretty sure
that Eyre Pomeroy would prove less amenable
to reason than his father expected him to be.
It is perhaps a mistake to be generous and
unsuspicious, and I myself may be too old to be
either the one or the other ; still I admire those
qualities in my juniors, and although, as I have
said, I had been a little disappointed in Madame
de Chanteloup for accepting Eyre, I should
have been still more disappointed in him if the
revelation which he was about to hear had
induced him to break with her. At the same
time, it will be readily understood that I did
not see my way to lending countenance or

encouragement to filial rebellion ; so that when, some hours later, my young friend was announced, I began at once by saying—

" If you have come here to ask me to intercede for·you with your father, you have come upon a vain errand. I warned you from the first, remember, that you would have trouble with him, and now you must fight your own battle."

" I haven't come upon any errand of that kind, Mr. Wortley," answered the young man gravely and sadly, " and there is no quarrel between me and the governor, who, I must say, has been as—as considerate as it was possible to be. More considerate, perhaps, than some other people."

His tone was so absolutely the reverse of what I had anticipated, that I was fairly taken aback, and, to tell the truth, rather angered into the bargain.

" Meaning me ? " I inquired.

" Well," answered the young man, seating

himself—and I noticed that there was a drawn look about his face, while all the healthy colour had deserted it—" I think you might have been more candid with me. I can't help saying that I think I might have been more candidly dealt with. If it had been a question of mere gossip, I should have had nothing to complain of; but I don't quite understand my having been allowed to remain in ignorance as to matters of fact."

" Why, God bless my soul, sir ! " I exclaimed (for in the days of my youth I had a hasty temper, of which some traces still linger within me), " do you venture to rebuke me because I didn't poke my nose into the byways of diplomacy in order to blacken the fair fame of the very best woman with whom I have the honour to be acquainted ? Who are you, pray, that I should stab a friend in the back to save you from committing an act of folly upon which you were bent ? You intend, I take it, to break faith with Madame de Chanteloup. Very well; only, if you are in any degree a gentleman, you will account for your abandonment of her by affirming what, I should think, was perfectly true—that your father's stalwart Protestantism won't admit of a matrimonial alliance between his heir and a Romanist."

The young fellow did not respond to my outburst by any counter-demonstration. "There is no use in using strong language, Mr. Wortley," said he, in the same calm, despairing voice. "I am as unhappy as you could possibly wish me to be; but I am not ashamed. If what my father has told me is true—and I am afraid that is beyond question—I can no more think of marrying the woman whom I love than I could think of disgracing myself and my family in any other way. Surely that must be obvious to you! And I don't think it would be honest on my part to give her any reason except the real one for what you call my abandonment of her."

He was undeniably and exasperatingly in the right. "As you please," I returned. "I can only say to you, as I have said to your father, that there is a doubt, and that, in my opinion, Madame de Chanteloup ought to be allowed the benefit of it. However, it really doesn't signify; because you don't mean to marry her—and, for the matter of that, I never believed that you would. And now, as I have an engagement to keep, and as I presume that you have nothing more to say, I will ask you to be so kind as to excuse me."

But it seemed that he had something more to say; it seemed—to put things coarsely—that he was desirous of employing me as a go-between, and that he thought I might spare him some pain by taking a message from him to Madame de Chanteloup. I need scarcely add that I emphatically declined to be employed in any such capacity.

" You have ridden at a fence which you are afraid to take," said I; " personally I don't care a straw whether you shirk it or break your neck over it. It is no business of mine to find you in courage, or to see you through difficulties."

"I must write to her, then," he replied, meekly. " You may call me a coward if you like; but I daren't trust myself to see her."

So he went his way; and I confess that, after he had departed, my conscience reproached me a little for the severity with which I had treated him. He was not really behaving so very badly; he really had been deceived, and I suppose it was the case that he owed some sacrifice of his personal inclinations to expediency and to the honour of the good old family whose name he bore. Still I could not forget my poor Countess's radiant face as I had seen it when she emerged from St. Germain

l'Auxerrois, and I could not for one instant
believe that she had ever been a bad woman,
though hard facts demonstrated that she had
been what, to all worldly intents and purposes,
is the same thing.

On the following afternoon I called at her
house. I can't exactly say what my object was
in so doing, nor had I any expectation that I
could be of the slightest use to her in her
distress ; but, having heard nothing of or from
young Pomeroy during the morning, and being
by no means sure that he would not leave
Paris without even bidding me good-bye, I
yielded to the feeling of restless uneasiness
which had oppressed me ever since the conclusion of my interview with him. If the
reader likes to assume that I was prompted by
mere vulgar curiosity, I make the reader
welcome to that assumption : it would not be
the first time that such a charge has been
brought against me.

Anyhow, my curiosity was not gratified, for I failed to obtain admission into Madame de Chanteloup's drawing-room. Madame la Comtesse, the servant informed me, was *très-souffrante;* she had had one of her bad neuralgic headaches all day, and had now gone to bed, giving orders that she was on no account to be disturbed until the evening. So I handed him my card, mentioned that I would return to make inquiries on the morrow, and went my way to the club, where I remained until the clock warned me that it was time to go home and dress for a dinner-party to which I had been bidden.

A *fiacre* was turning away from my door just as I reached it, and when I was about half-way upstairs I overtook Eyre Pomeroy, who was clinging to the banisters and who seemed scarcely able to put one foot before another.

" What is the matter ? " I exclaimed, taking

him by the arm ; " what has happened ? "—for
I saw by his ghastly face that some catastrophe
must have occurred.

" What has happened ? " he repeated, in a
strange thick voice. " Haven't you heard ?—
no, of course you haven't. She is dead, that's
all—yes, *dead!* I don't know whether you
can believe it or not; *I* can't, though there
isn't a doubt about its being true."

To the best of my recollection, I did not
believe it. I thought the lad must have been
drinking, or that he was the victim of some
hallucination. He was, at all events, incapable
of expressing himself coherently. It was only
after I had got him into an arm-chair and had
made him swallow a couple of glasses of wine
that he recovered the use of his tongue ; and
even then he remained so painfully agitated
that I had difficulty in understanding what
he said. I gathered, however, that he had, on
the previous evening, written such a letter to

Madame de Chanteloup as he had intimated his intention of writing.

"I received her answer," he said, "an hour —or perhaps it was two hours' ago. Here it is; read it, and you will see—you will see—— "

His voice broke, and it was some seconds before he could resume: "Of course, I rushed at once to her house. There was a great disturbance there. I didn't understand what it was about; but they tried to keep me back, and I forced my way in. All the doors were open; the servants were in her bedroom, sobbing and chattering; I think there was a policeman there too; I saw her lying on the bed, dead and cold. She had been ill and had taken an over-dose of chloral, they said. I think I had better kill myself too; for you will see by her letter that she was innocent and that I murdered her!"

I quieted him as best I could; but naturally

"ALL THE DOORS WERE OPEN; THE SERVANTS WERE IN HER BEDROOM, SOBBING
AND CHATTERING; I THINK THERE WAS A POLICEMAN THERE TOO; I SAW
HER LYING ON THE BED, DEAD AND COLD."

I myself was somewhat overcome, and even if I had had all my wits about me I don't know that I could have said very much to comfort him. Presently he sank back in his chair and motioned to me to read the letter which he had placed in my hand.

I need not quote the whole of it; indeed, I am not sure that, had he been calmer, he would have cared to let me see the opening sentences, which conveyed an assurance of such passionate love as I should scarcely have supposed Madame de Chanteloup capable of penning, and which, even at that sad moment, I could not help wondering at his having had the power to arouse. But, notwithstanding this—or possibly on account of it—the writer acquiesced without a murmur in the sentence which had been pronounced against her, acknowledging that it was inevitable, and only marvelling that she had ever imagined that it might be averted.

"Still," she added, "now that all is over between us, and since you cannot, I think, suspect me of any wish to bring you back to me, I should like you to know that the truth is not quite so bad as you have been led to believe. The Prince paid me great attentions, and my vanity was flattered by them; I liked him very much, though I did not love him; I was scarcely more than a child; I knew nothing of the world, and when he used to talk about a morganatic marriage I saw no impossibility in such an arrangement. Indeed, so far as I had any voice in the matter, I had consented to this when, all of a sudden, I was told that he had gone away, that I should never see him again, that he had even been placed under a sort of arrest, and—that I was to marry M. de Chanteloup. Of course I was very unhappy; but I had always been completely under the control of my mother, who told me this was not a case for argument, that

she had done the very best she could for me,
and that I must bow to necessity. It was not
until after my marriage that I learnt from my
husband by what infamous means the trans-
action which handed me over to him had been
brought about. I don't speak of my mother's
share in it. She was ambitious; in her eager-
ness to make what she considered a magnificent
alliance for me she probably committed herself
to false statements which may afterwards have
been used against her, and from which she
could find no honourable way of escape. At
any rate, my husband's revelation came far
too late to save or serve me. If I had pro-
claimed my true story from the house-tops,
not one person in a thousand would have
believed it. But *you*, I hope, will believe it,
and forgive the wrong I was so nearly doing
you, as I have forgiven those who have ruined
my life."

There was a good deal more; but I could

4

only glance at the remainder of the letter; for young Pomeroy had started up from his recumbent attitude, and his cold, trembling fingers were laid upon my wrist.

"Well?" said he, impatiently. "Speak out—don't be afraid of hurting me. Do you think she did it?"

I was astonished at the question. "Why,' I exclaimed, "you yourself told me just now that you were persuaded of her innocence, and I must confess—— "

"No, no!" he interrupted, fretfully; "you don't understand me. As if I would let you dare to cast a doubt upon her innocence! What I mean is, do you—do you think she killed herself?"

I could only say, as I had said in a previous instance, that I thought she should be allowed the benefit of the doubt. That is all that I can say or think now; and although Eyre Pomeroy would have been better pleased, I suppose,

if I could have given him the more positive
assurance which he craved, he did not, pre-
sumably, consider that the circumstances would
justify him in fulfilling his own threat of
self-destruction.

Far from acting so foolishly and wickedly,
he has lately gratified his family by making
a highly satisfactory marriage, and I should
not imagine that he has revisited Père Lachaise
since the dismal, rainy day when he followed
poor Madame de Chanteloup's remains to their
last resting-place in that dreariest of all burial
grounds.

A MEMORABLE SWIM.

By W. CLARK RUSSELL.

THE little sitting-room, at whose open window I was seated, was very hot; from the lodgings on either hand there broke into the quietude of the night a horrid, distracting noise of jingling pianos, accompanied by a squealing of female voices. The hour was about eleven. I filled my pipe afresh, left the house, and walked in the direction of the beach.

The moon rode high; I had never before seen the orb so small and also so brilliantly piercing; she diffused a wide haze of greenish

W. CLARK RUSSELL.

silver round about her in the heavens, in the skirts of which a few stars of magnitude shone sparely, though, clear of the sphere of this steam-like radiance, the sky trembled with brilliants, and went hovering to the sea-line, rich with prisms and crystals. In the heart of the silent ocean lay the fan-shaped wake of the moon, and the splendour of its hither extremity, so wide-reaching was it, seemed to melt in the lines of summer surf, which formed and dissolved upon the wet-darkened sand.

It wanted about a quarter of an hour to the turn of the ebb. The sands were a broad, firm platform, and stretched before and behind me, whitened into the complexion of ivory by the moonbeams. The cliffs rose tall and dark on my left, a silent range of iron terraces, with the black sky-line of them showing out against the stars, and with nothing to break their continuity save here and there a gap, as of some ravine. The summer-night hush was

exquisitely soothing.   From afar came the thin,
faint notes of a band of music playing in the
town, past the huge shoulder of cliff, but the
distance was too great to suffer the strains to
vex the ear; indeed, the silence was accen-
tuated rather than disturbed by that far-off
music.   The creeping of the surf was like the
voice of innumerable fountains.   There was
not a breath of air; the moon's reflections lay
tremorless; and in the liquid dusk on the
western edge of that motionless path of light.
floated the phantom shape of a ship, her hull
as black as ink, and her sails stirlessly poised
over her, like ice in shadow.

I walked dreamily onwards, smoking my
pipe, and listening to the innumerable babble
of the waters upon the beach.   I went perhaps
a mile.   There was plenty of time; no hurry
to go to bed on such a night, and there would
be abundance of room for the walk home, long
after the tide should have turned.

I came abreast of a mass of black rock, table-
shaped, and nearly awash ; that is to say, the
water stood almost at the level of it, so that
at flood it would be submerged and out of
sight. I spied what I thought to be a gleam
of light resting upon it ; but on looking again
I was sure that that strange shining could
not be moonlight, for the lustre was local,
and it was not light either, but white, and
its size was about that of a man's body ; and,
indeed, it looked so much like a naked man
that I drew close to examine it. There was
dry sand to the rock ; but the water brimmed
very nearly around it, and there was water
under where the white object lay. On drawing
near, I observed that what I had thought to
be a gleam of light was the body of a drowned
man. I stood staring long enough to satisfy
me that he was dead. It was a dismal and
a dreadful object to light upon. The very
silence of the night, the beauty of the stars,

the high, peaceful, piercing moon somehow increased the horror of the thing. On a dark, stormy night, I do not know that such a spectacle would have so shocked and unnerved me as this now did.

I peered to right and left, but not the shadow of mortal being stirred upon the white sweep of the sands. Then, casting my eyes up at the cliff, I recollected that a little distance further on there was a gully, at the head of which stood a coastguard's hut, and, knowing that there would be a man stationed on the look-out up there, I forthwith bent my steps in the direction of the gully, and ascended it, until I arrived at the hut. Here I found a coastguard. He eyed me fixedly as I approached him.

I said, " Good night, coastguard."

" Good night," he answered, attentively surveying me by the light of the moon.

" I am somewhat breathless," said I; " I have

walked fast, and that gully is hard to climb. There is a dead body down on the beach."

" Whereabouts, sir ? " he exclaimed with the instant promptitude of the seaman, and he advanced to the edge of the cliff.

" It lies on that rock there," said I, pointing.

" I see it, sir," said he. " D'ye mind coming along with me? My mate won't be here for a bit."

Together we proceeded to the sands. The coastguard got upon the rock and stood viewing the body. Then, catching hold of it by the arms, he dragged it gently on to the sand.

" Ay," said he; " I thought as much. This'll be the gent as was drowned whilst bathing out of a boat yesterday. Poor fellow! he's left a wife and two children. There's been a reward of twenty pounds offered for his body. That'll be yourn, sir."

" It will be yours," said I. " I do not stand in need of money earned in this fashion."

The body was that of a man of about thirty. He had fair hair and a large moustache, and in life had doubtless been a handsome young fellow.

" 'Tain't often as they comes ashore so perfect," said the coastguard. " They're mostly all ate up so as to be unrecognizable."

I recoiled, and said, " Why am I afraid of this body? It cannot hurt me. It is but a dead man, and comely too. Why, as he lies there, coastguard, he might be formed of ivory, moulded by the fingers of the sea out of its own foam, and cast up thus. And yet," said I, looking round with a silly, chilly shiver running through me, " I believe it would go near to unsettling my wits were I forced to stand watch by this body all through the night here."

" I see he's got his rings on," said the matter-of-fact coastguard, stooping to bring his eyes close to the fingers of the body.

" What is now to be done?" said I.

" Which way might you be going, sir?"

" Home—back to the town," I replied; " I've walked enough by the sea-shore to-night."

" Then," said the coastguard, " I'll ask you to report this here discovery to the first bobby ye meets with. Tell him that the body lies almost abreast of Dowton Gap; and, if you don't mind giving me a hand, sir, to carry the corpse to the foot of the cliff, in case the bobby—the tide ye see——"

" No," said I; " you dragged it single-handed from the rock. You are able to drag it single-handed to the foot of the cliff. If I touched the poor thing—well, good night, coastguard," and I walked off, leaving him to handle the dead body single-handed, for which I had no better excuse to make than that I was possessed at the time by strong feelings of horror, and perhaps fear, which the presence of the coastguard in no degree mitigated, and which were induced, as I can now believe, by the suddenness and violence of the obtrusion of an object of terror upon my mind at a moment when it had been rendered in a peculiar sense unprepared for any such experience by the enervating charm, the sweet relaxing magic of the soft and glorious night of moonshine and silence, and waters seething with the stealthy hiss of champagne.

I stepped out briskly, and as I walked I seemed to behold many white bodies of drowned men floating shorewards on the summer feathering of the little breakers. When I arrived at the town I met a policeman, to whom I communicated the news, and I then returned to my lodgings and sat in the open window smoking a pipe, and as I lighted my pipe the clocks in the town struck the hour of midnight.

As I sat smoking thus, I surrendered my

mind so wholly to contemplation of the dead white body I had suddenly fallen in with, that I might well have supposed the impression which the encounter would leave must be life-long. But next day I returned to London, and within a week the memory of the little incident had as good as perished from my mind. For a month I was very busy. My employment was exceedingly arduous, and often obliged me to work late into the night. Then, at the expiration of the month, feeling uncommonly fagged, I resolved to spend a week at the same seaside town where I had discovered the body on the rock.

The name of this town I will not give. I do not wish to excite the anger of its boatmen. "Ho!" they will say, should I name their town. "Ho!" they will cry when they have arrived at the end of my story, "what a loy! This here piece is put into the newspapers all along o' spite. The gent don't wish us

well, and he's invented this here blooming
yarn to scare folks from employing of us.
He's agoing to start a pleasure yacht for taking
o' people out at a shilling a head, and don't
mean that us pore watermen shall get a living."
Thus would you declaim, oh, ye sons of the
beach; and that you may in no wise suffer
from any statements of mine, I withhold the
name of your town, so that the reader may
take his choice of any port or harbour on the
coast of the United Kingdom.   Nevertheless,
what I am about to relate is no " loy," but the
truth itself—absolute, memorable, living.

I was again at the seaside.   It was now the
month of August, and the hottest August that
I can remember.   After the intolerable heat of
London, and the fatigue of my work there,
nothing, of course, could prove so beneficial,
so bracing, in all senses so restoring, as sea-
bathing.   But for the bathing-machine sea-bath
I had the strongest aversion.   First, there was

no depth of water for swimming. The necessary
depth for true enjoyment was to be gained only
when the limbs were well-nigh exhausted by
the labour of striking out for it. Then I
disliked to bathe in company. Again, I
objected to the crowds who stood watching the
bathers from the piers and sands. In fact, for
an expert swimmer, such as I, there is but one
method of bathing in the sea : he must take a
boat, row out a mile or two where the brine
sparkles foamless, where it is clear of the con-
tamination of the set of the inshore tide, where
the blue or green of it is darkly pure with depth.

On the morning following the day of my
arrival, somewhere about the hour of seven
o'clock, I threw some towels over my arm and
walked down to a part of the harbour where I
knew I should find a boatman. Even at this
early hour the bite of the sun was as fierce as
though he stood at his meridian. The atmosphere was of a brilliant blue. There was a

little air of wind that delicately rippled the sea. I beheld not a cloud in the sky—no, not so much as a shred of vapour of the size of a man's hand. In the harbour the red canvas of smacks preparing to go to sea painted the water under them. The soft wind brought many wholesome odours of tar, of sea-weed, of sawn timber to the nostrils. As I approached that part of the pier off which most of the wherries belonging to the town were congregated, a man who was leaning with his back to me over a stone post, gazing in the direction of the sands, turned his head, and, guessing at my intention, by observing the towels I carried, stood erect with alacrity, and called out " Boat, sir ? The werry morning for a swim, sir. A sheet calm, and the flood's only now agoing to make."

Though I had from time to time visited the town, I had never spent more than three days at a time in it; and the boatmen, therefore, were strangers to me. I said to this man :—

" Yes, it is the very morning for a swim.
What sort of a boat is yours ? "

" The best boat in the harbour, sir," he answered. " There she lies, sir—a real beauty,"
and he pointed eagerly at a wherry painted
blue, with raised tholepins, after the fashion of
the boats of the Thames watermen.

I looked at her and said, " Yes, she will do
very well to take a header from. Bring her
alongside."

It was not until I was seated in the stern-
sheets of the boat that I particularly noticed
this waterman, who, having flung his oars over,
was propelling his little craft through the water
with a velocity that was warrant of an extra-
ordinarily powerful arm. My eyes then resting
upon his face, I found myself struck by his
uncommon appearance. His skin was very dark,
his hair jet-black, and his eyes were of a glassy
brilliance, with pupils of jet. Coarse as his hair
was, it curled in ringlets. He wore a pair of

5

immensely thick whiskers, every fibre of which might have been plucked from a horse's tail. His nose was heavy and large, and the curve of the nostrils very deeply graven. In each ear was a thick gold hoop, and the covering of his head consisted of a cap fashioned out of a skin. Otherwise he was habited in the familiar garb of the British boatman—in a blue jersey, large loose trousers, of a yellow stuff called "fearnaught;" top-boots under the trousers, which were turned up to reveal a portion of the leather. I observed that his gaze had an odd character of staring ; it was fixed, stern, yet with a suggestion of restlessness in it, as of temper.

" Are you a Jew ? " said I.

" No fear," he answered.

" Do not suppose that I ask the question out of any disrespect to you. The Jews are a very intelligent, interesting people. It would cause me to wonder, however, to find a Jew a boatman."

"I ain't no Jew, sir," said he.

" Perhaps you are what is called a Romany Chal ? "

" What's that ? " he cried, gazing at me with his staring eyes.

" A gipsy, isn't it ? "

He grinned, and answered, " Well, I believe I has some pikey blood in me."

" What do you mean by pikey ? "

" Gipsy," said he.

" That must be a local term," said I, " probably derived from the word 'turnpike,' as connecting the gipsies with the road."

He strained at his oars in silence ; but my questions appeared to have excited some curiosity in him as to myself, for I observed that he ran his eyes over me, dwelling with attention upon every part of my apparel, more especially, as it struck me, upon the rings upon my fingers, and upon my watch chain.

I stood up to look around. We were clear of

the harbour ; and the fine scene of the cliffs,
the houses on top, with their flashing windows,
the white lustrous line of sands, lay stretched
before my sight.   We were the only small boat
upon the surface of the sea; but near the pier
were a number of bathing-machines, and several
dark knots of heads like cocoanuts bobbed in
the snow-bright lines of the surf.   The horizon
was broken by the outlines of a few vessels, and
one large steamer gliding stately and resplen-
dent, flashes of white fire, like exploding guns,
breaking from the double line of her glazed
portholes as her movements brought those
windows to the sun, gleams of ruddy flame
leaping from the polished brass furniture about
her bridge, and a long line of water glancing
astern of her, as though she towed from her
sternpost some league-long length of shimmer-
ing white satin.

   " What might be the correct time, sir ? "
asked the boatman.

I drew out my watch, a handsome gold repeater, and gave him the hour. He thanked me, and said, "I suppose you're a good swimmer, sir?"

"I am a very good swimmer," I answered.

"Then the deeper the water, the better you'll be pleased, sir. I've been told that arter six fadom of water every furder fadom makes a man feel so much more buoyant that it's like strapping a fresh bladder on to him."

"No doubt," said I. "What depths have you here?"

"Oh, here," cried he, contemptuously glancing over the side, "why, there ain't twelve foot of water here. We're right on top of a bank. Ye'll need to let me pull you about a mile and a half out to get the soundings you want for a first-class swim."

"Well," said I, "there is no hurry. You know all about these waters, of course? By the way, when I was here a month ago I found a drowned body on the sands down there."

"Oh, was you the gent, then, as fell in with that body?" said the man, regarding me with his peculiar gipsy stare. "There was a matter of twenty pound offered for that discovery. Wish *I'd* had the finding of the poor fellow. Twenty pound. Only think. And it was all paid over to a coastguard."

"That's right," said I. "I walked up that break in the cliffs yonder to the coastguard's hut there and gave notice. Who was the drowned man, do you know?"

"It came out in the cronner's 'quest, but I forget the name."

"How was he drowned?"

"Why, by awading out of his depth, I allow."

"The coastguard told me he was drowned by bathing from a boat."

"He didn't know nothen about it," answered the boatman. "There never yet was a man drownded by bathing out of a boat in these parts. Didn't ye see the account of the 'quest in the newspapers?"

"No."

"Well," said the man, "it was supposed he was took with cramp. There's too many drownding jobs of that sort going on along the coast. It don't do us watermen any good. It creates a prejudice agin the places where the accidents happen. What does a man want to go out of his depth for if he ain't no swimmer?"

We fell silent, and he continued to row with great energy, whilst I lay back in the stern-sheets enjoying the sweet cool freshness of the salt air breathing upon the face of the waters, and greatly enjoying the noble and brilliant spectacle of the sea shining under the sun, and of the coast, whose many colours, and whose many features of structure, of elbow, of cliff, of green slope, of down on top, every stroke

of the oar was now making more tender, more
delicate, more toy-like.

After rowing for about twenty minutes, the
gipsy-faced boatman rested upon his oars, and,
taking a look round, and then gazing over the
side into the water, he exclaimed, " This here'll
be the spot, sir."

I at once undressed, stood up in the stern-
sheets, put my hands together, and went overboard into the cool, green, glass-clear profound.
I came to the surface, and, with a shake of the
head, cleared my eyes, and perceived the boatman very leisurely pulling his wherry still
further out to sea. This was, perhaps, as it
should be. He might, indeed, have headed his
boat in for the land; but, in any case, he was
right to keep her in motion as an invitation
to me to swim after her. I swam with great
enjoyment; the embrace of the water pene-
trated to my inmost being, and every pulse
in me beat with a new vitality. I swam

directly in the wake of the boat, past the rim
of whose stern I could see the head of the boatman. He held me in view, and he watched
me intently, though from time to time he
would direct his gaze to that part of the land
where the town was situated, and sometimes
he would turn his head and look behind him—
that is to say, over the bows of his boat, in the
manner of one who cannot satisfy himself that
something is not approaching.

Presently, I thought I would catch hold of
the boat by the gunwale to rest myself, and
I called to him to stop rowing, that I might
come up with him; but he did not stop rowing.
When I called he turned his face from me, and
continued to ply his oars. I called to him
again, but he paid no attention to me. There
was the sullen air of murder in his averted
face, and in his whole manner of determination
not to hear me. My heart beat furiously, and
I felt faint, for *now*, with the velocity of

thought, I was linking the fate of the man
whose dead body I had lighted upon with the
gipsy ruffian ahead of me in the boat; and I
said to myself, he might have been drowned,
and perhaps by that very demon there, as I

"I CALLED TO HIM TO STOP ROWING, THAT I MIGHT COME UP TO
HIM; BUT HE DID NOT STOP ROWING.

am to be drowned; left, as I am to be left, to
swim until he sank from exhaustion, as I am
to sink, that the boatman might possess himself of his watch and chain and money, as my

watch and chain and money are the objects for which I am to be obliged to struggle here until I perish.

These thoughts swept with the speed of a dream through my head. I cried aloud in a voice of bitter despair—as acutely realizing now the murderous villain's intention as though I had spent an hour in digesting it—"For God's sake, do not leave me here to drown. Take what you want; take all that I have. Have mercy upon me. Let me reach your boat and rest!"

He continued to row, with his face averted from me, and I was near enough to him to easily observe the villainous, diabolical expression that now sat upon his dark countenance as he stared in silence towards the land. I turned upon my back to rest myself, and all the while my feverishly-beating heart seemed to be saying, "What is to be done? Must you drown? You are not two miles from the shore. Cannot you swim that distance? Rest awhile on your back, and then strike out like a man. You have no other chance for your life. That demon yonder intends that you shall drown. He will secrete the booty he means to take out of your pockets, and will row ashore and put on a face of consternation, and report that when you were overboard you were seized with cramp, and sank on a sudden like a stone."

Whilst I thus lay upon my back, besieged by the most dreadful thoughts, half mad with wrath and with despair, the boatman sculled back to me, and, putting the blade of his left oar upon my breast, thrust with it with the idea of submerging me. I grasped the oar, and held it with the tenacity of a dying man. He could not shake me off; his right oar slipped from his hand and went overboard; the boat swayed dangerously. My desire, indeed, was to capsize it, because I should have the ruffian

"——AND, PUTTING THE BLADE OF HIS LEFT OAR UPON MY BREAST, THRUST WITH IT WITH THE IDEA OF SUBMERGING ME."

at an advantage if I could get him into the water, heavily clad as he was, even though he should be as expert a swimmer as I; and then there would be the boat to hold to, because, being light and without ballast, even if she filled she would not sink; furthermore, there was the certainty of our situation being witnessed from the coast, and of help being despatched forthwith.

It might have been that he feared the boat would capsize, and it might have been that he guessed we should be presently observed through some telescope levelled at us from the pier or cliff. He suddenly cried with a furious curse, "Get in, get in!" and, letting go his oar, he dragged me into the boat, flinging me from him, so that I fell over an after thwart, and lay for a few moments breathless, and almost unconscious, in the bottom of the boat. He then threw his oar over and manœuvred the wherry, so as to recover the other oar, which done, he adjusted himself on his seat and fell to rowing on a course parallel with the coast.

I rose, trembling in every limb; the shock had been terrible; my rescue a miracle. I seemed to feel the hand of death cold upon my heart, even as I staggered on to my feet; and still I was in dire peril—alone with a powerful, muscular ruffian, who, having already attempted my life, might again, in self-defence, to silence my testimony against him, renew his murderous effort in another direction. With an exhausted hand I passed a towel over my body and then clothed myself. Meanwhile, not a word was uttered. The man eyed me with ferocity, and his under-lip moved as though he were rehearsing some thoughts to himself in an impish jargon. We still continued to be the only boat upon the water. The great steamer had long since passed out of sight, and upon the horizon hung the few sails, scarcely impelled by the languid breath of the air that was slowly weakening as the sun gained in power.

At last I said to the man, " Where are you going ? "

" That's my business," he answered.

" Where are you taking me to ? " I exclaimed.

He fastened his staring, gleaming eyes upon me and answered, " I'm going to put ye ashore."

" But you are not rowing the boat in the direction of the town."

" I know I'm not."

" I want you to set me ashore at the place where we started from."

" Ye *may* want," he replied, pausing upon his oars to advance his head towards me as he spoke, as though, in another moment, he would leap upon me.

By this time I had rallied my wits somewhat. The feeling of profound exhaustion was also passing. I was dressed, and the mere being

dressed was in its way a help towards the
composure of the mind. I was man to man
with the ruffian, but not his match—no, I had
but to run my eye over his figure to understand
that. I sat contemplating his villainous face
and thinking. There was a boat-stretcher at
my feet; but the man's fierce, keen eye was
upon me; before I could grasp and employ
the stretcher, the fellow would have guessed
my intentions, and I must therefore either sit
still and wait until I could understand what
he meant to do, or fling myself upon him and
take the chance of being hurled overboard.
No purpose could be served by my capsizing
the boat. I was now clothed, and my movements in the water would, therefore, be
seriously hampered; and then, again, if I engaged in a struggle, with the intention of
capsizing the boat, and succeeded in doing so,
it might be his fortune to regain her and to
keep me off from her, and, apparelled and

exhausted as I was, I should not long be able to remain afloat.

He continued to row along a course that was still parallel with the coast. He rowed with a sort of sulky energy, and often directed a furious look at me, whilst his leather nether lip worked as though he were reciting some charm to himself. Presently I said to him, "Where are you taking me to? Why will you not put me ashore where we started from? You have tried to drown me, and your object can be nothing but plunder, for I have not offended you, I have done you no wrong, and, therefore, your only reason for attempting to drown me must be the jewellery upon me, and such money as you may hope I have in my pocket. Now, I will give you all that I possess—my watch and chain, this ring, and the two or three pounds which I have in my pocket—if you will set me ashore where I came from."

He stared fiercely at me, but made no response.

6

" Do you fear I will charge you with the crime you have attempted ? " said I. " If you will set me ashore in safety I swear not to say a word upon what has happened."

" I'm going to set ye ashore," he exclaimed.

" But where ? "

He flung his villainous head backwards towards the sea over the bows of his boat and said, " You'll be finding out afore long."

" Ah," thought I, " if I had but a revolver in my pocket, if I had but a knife, if I had but any sort of weapon that I could furtively draw forth and instantly employ ! "

The line of coast ran away down on the left-hand side. The nearest town in the direction the boatman was taking would be some miles distant from the place in which I was staying. The cliffs gradually rose to an altitude of hard upon a hundred feet, with many indents and little coves ; but the face of them, as we advanced, grew more and yet more precipitous,

and in places the rocks stood abrupt and clean
as the side of a wall. When the harbour ι
had quitted was out of sight, and the fiιaι
group of houses on our side was hidden by the
bend of the cliffs, the boatman took a swift look
over his shoulder, then slightly changed the
course of his boat, making her head in for the
coast to a sort of bight of it, as it seemed,
formed by an angular projection of the huge,
iron-faced sea-terrace, so that it looked as
if the land ended where that point of coast
stood, for the horizon went to it, and we were
not far enough out to see the sweep of land
beyond.

That the boatman designed some diabolical
act I did not doubt, but I could not imagine
what form it was to take. He meant to set me
ashore, he said. Did he intend to land and
then murder me; to land me in some lonely
bight or cave, and there fall upon me, and slay
me? No, I did not believe that. If he in-

tended to make away with me for the sake of my money and jewellery, it would be his business to provide that I should appear to have been drowned by accident. Otherwise, how would he account for my disappearance? Or, if my body should be discovered, and marks of a devilish outrage were visible upon it, what answer would he be able to make to the charge of having murdered me?

But what then did he mean to do? To set me ashore? In that case I should be able to walk home and report what had happened. Did *he* mean to return to the town that he belonged to? That could not signify, for let him make for any port that he chose his capture was ultimately certain.

He swept the boat in rapidly to the coast, heading her for a curvature in the land that might have passed for a miniature bay. The sea remained a blank, save for those dim and distant sails upon the horizon. The water washed to the foot of the coast; but in the little bay, for which the villain was aiming, I could perceive, as the boat rose on the slight swell that was now running, the gleam of sand. Nothing stirred on the heights; we were now within a quarter of a mile, but not a moving object was visible. He continued to row until the boat was in the embrace of the bay. The dark cliffs soared like a colossal rampart to high overhead, and at either extremity of the curve of the bay, at the point of either horn of it, there was a little play of surf. The man flung in his oars and stood up.

"Give me that watch and chain of yourn!" he shouted.

I rose to my feet.

"Give me that watch and chain," he roared again, and thrusting his great dark hand into his breeches pocket he whipped out a big clasp knife, which he opened. "No trouble," he exclaimed, "or I'll cut your throat."

I placed the watch and chain down upon a thwart, and he pocketed them.

" Now pull out all the money you have."

This I did, and he took the coins and put them in his pocket.

" Pull off that ring."

This I also did. He eyed me all over, still grasping the knife. Then looking towards the beach, he said, " That's where I'm going to land ye. You're a good swimmer. Jump overboard."

" If you land me there," said I, " I shall be drowned. The water is rising, and those rocks are not to be climbed."

" Jump overboard ! " said he, with a menacing flourish of his knife.

" It is a bit of a swim as yet," said I. " I am sick and without strength. For God's sake put me a little closer to the beach that I may have a chance ! "

He hesitated a moment, then stooped to pick

"IN THAT INSTANT I BOUNDED UPON HIM."

up an oar. In that instant I bounded upon
him. Impelled by the incommunicable agony
of mind I was in, by what I may truly call the
terrific impulse of the despair that was upon
me, I leapt the thwart with the velocity of a
wolf at full cry, and ere he could lift his eyes
I had put my shoulder to his side, and hove
him into the water. Shipping an oar, I pulled
the boat's head round, shipped the other oar
betwixt the thole-pins, and pulled out of the
bay with all my might.

Before the point of cliffs had shut out
the bay, I caught sight of his head. The
fellow was swimming, and swimming strongly,
towards the curve of the sand at the foot of
the cliff. I now understood the sort of fate he
had intended for me. Having gained the sand,
I should have been imprisoned by the water ;
but the tide was making fast, and, when the
flood was at its full, the sea-line stood some feet
above the level of the sand. There was not

an accessible piece of jutting rock—nothing for
the hand to grasp, nor for the foot to support
itself by, upon the face of the perpendicular
steep.   Therefore I must inevitably have been
drowned.   And what story would the ruffian
have invented to account for my disappearance?
I conceived this: that he would have leisurely
rowed back to the harbour, moored his boat,
and lounged upon the pier, as his custom was,
without uttering a syllable about me, unless,
indeed, he had been observed to row me out
in his boat in the morning, and should be asked
what had become of me.   Supposing this question asked, he would answer that at my request
he had set me ashore some two or three miles
down the coast, as I desired to walk home by
way of the cliffs.   Who could have disproved
this?   It must have been readily credited.   It
was a thing that was again and again happening.   And now imagine my body found upon
the sands of the little bay where he had com-

pelled me to swim ashore! There would have
been an inquest; it would be ascertained that
I was the gentleman whom the gipsy boatman
had set ashore. What more probable, then,
than that I should have changed my mind,
have attempted to make my way home in my
ignorance of the neighbourhood, by way of the
beach, instead of by way of the cliffs, and so
have perished?

These thoughts occupied my mind as I rowed
the wherry in the direction of the harbour. I
pulled at the oars with fury; I was sensible of
a horrid distraction of fear, as though it were
in the power of the ruffian to pursue me, to
arrest the boat, to enter her and cut my throat
with the knife he had flourished. I entered
the harbour, sculled to a landing stage, secured
the painter of the boat to it, and stepped
ashore. There were many people about; the
air resounded with the cries of boatmen inviting
the passers-by to go out for a row or a sail.

None of these men took any notice of me. Probably none of them knew that I had started in company with the gipsy boatman, and they would probably imagine that I had returned from a solitary pull out to sea. I walked a little way, and presently observed a harbour police-man. I approached him, and said—

"I want to inform against a ruffian who has just attempted my life."

He looked me hard in the face, and was clearly impressed by my agitation and appearance.

"What's wrong?" said he.

"A boatman whom I went out with this morning has attempted to drown me," said I.

"Step this way, sir," said the man; and with that he conducted me to a brick-built house adjoining a row of warehouses, and in the window of this brick-built house was a large wire blind, on which was wrought in golden letters the words, "Harbour Police

Office." The policeman lifted the latch of the door and entered, and I followed him. An immense man, with large, red whiskers, wearing a sort of naval cap with letters interwreathed over the peak of it, and a frock-coat, the breast of which was braided, sat upon a tall, three-legged stool reading a newspaper. He looked at me over his spectacles as I entered.

"Here's a gent says that one of the boatmen's been a-trying to drown him," said the policeman ; and, addressing me, he added, "This is the superintendent."

The superintendent put down his paper and took off his glasses, and asked me to tell him my business. I forthwith related my experiences to him. He listened attentively, occasionally glancing at the constable, who stood by listening with his mouth slightly open.

"Describe the man, sir," said the superintendent.

I did so.

"It's Gipsy Bill," said the constable.

"Yes, it's Gipsy Bill," said the superintendent—"the same man as took out the party
that was drowned last month."

"And the same man," said the constable,

"HE LISTENED ATTENTIVELY, OCCASIONALLY GLANCING AT THE CON-
STABLE, WHO STOOD BY LISTENING WITH HIS MOUTH SLIGHTLY OPEN."

"as took out the party that was drowned a year
ago come next month."

The superintendent thumped his leg. "I've
been suspicious of that chap all through," said

he. " Freeman, call Jones and Woodward, and take the boat and get the man. The flood'll not be at its height yet, and the man himself'll be as prettily nailed as though we had him in the lock-up."

I heard him pronounce these words, then a blood-red blaze of fire seemed to rush from my brain out through my eyes. I fell, and remember no more.

When I recovered my consciousness I was in bed in my own lodgings. All necessary information about me had been found in my pocket, in the shape of letters and cards. My sister had been telegraphed for, and she was at my bedside when I awoke, after three days of utter insensibility. When I was strong enough to listen and converse, I was told that the police-boat had pulled down to the little bay, found the man, and brought him to the town, where he was lying, locked up, charged with the attempt to murder me. Confirmatory proofs

of his guilt, outside the story I had related to
the superintendent, were found upon his person,
for the demon, probably forgetting in his time
of peril that he had pocketed my watch and
chain, my ring, and my money, had omitted
to conceal them or fling them away when the
police-boat showed herself round the corner.

But this was not all ; two visitors had lost
their lives within a year. The body of one
only was recovered, and this was the poor
fellow whose remains I had stumbled upon
during my lonely moonlight walk along the
sands. It was believed that both these men
had perished whilst bathing from a boat, and
the coroner, during the inquest held upon the
body that had been recovered, had commented
somewhat significantly upon the circumstance
of both these disasters having occurred from
the same boat, in charge of the same man.

And now, whilst I had lain unconscious, the
police had searched the little house, or room,

occupied by the boatman named Gipsy Bill, and there they had discovered a gold pencil-case and a pair of gold pince-nez glasses and a watch-chain, of which articles the two former were claimed as belonging to the man who had been drowned in the previous year, whilst the watch-chain was sworn to by the widow of the gentle-man whose body I had discovered, the poor lady happening to be in the town whilst I lay unconscious. The upshot of it was that Gipsy Bill was sentenced to penal servitude for life. That he was guilty of two murders was certain, and therefore he ought to have been hanged. Nevertheless, the circumstantial evidence did not seem sufficiently strong to admit of the death penalty, for it could not certainly be proved that the fiend, when his victims had plunged overboard, had quietly continued to row, leaving the unhappy men to sink with exhaustion in his wake. It could not certainly be proved that the poor fellows had *not* been

seized with cramp and suddenly sunk; but, all
the same, no one who heard the story ever
doubted that this demon of a gipsy boatman
had left them to perish, or, as he had attempted in my case, had hastened their end by
a blow with his oar.

TO PLEASE HIS WIFE.

By THOMAS HARDY.

I.

THOMAS HARDY.

THE interior of St. James's Church, in Havenpool Town, was slowly darkening under the close clouds of a winter afternoon. It was Sunday: service had just ended, the face of the parson in the pulpit was buried in his hands, and the congregation, with a cheerful sigh of release, were rising from their knees to depart.

For the moment the stillness was so complete

7

that the surging of the sea could be heard outside the harbour-bar. Then it was broken by the footsteps of the clerk going towards the west door to open it in the usual manner for the exit of the assembly. Before, however, he had reached the doorway, the latch was lifted from without, and the dark figure of a man in a sailor's garb appeared against the light.

The clerk stepped aside, the sailor closed the door gently behind him, and advanced up the nave till he stood at the chancel step. The parson looked up from the private little prayer which, after so many for the parish, he quite fairly took for himself, rose to his feet, and stared at the intruder.

"I beg your pardon, sir," said the sailor, addressing the minister in a voice distinctly audible to all the congregation. "I have come here to offer thanks for my narrow escape from shipwreck. I am given to

understand that it is a proper thing to do,
if you have no objection ? "

The parson, after a moment's pause, said
hesitatingly, "I have no objection; certainly.
It is usual to mention any such wish before
service, so that the proper words may be
used in the General Thanksgiving. But, if
you wish, we can read from the form for
use after a storm at sea."

" Ay, sure ; I ain't particular," said the sailor.

The clerk thereupon directed the sailor to
the page in the Prayer-book where the collect
of thanksgiving would be found, and the
rector began reading it, the sailor kneeling
where he stood, and repeating it after him
word by word in a distinct voice. The people,
who had remained agape and motionless at
the proceeding, mechanically knelt down like-
wise ; but they continued to regard the isolated
form of the sailor who, in the precise middle
of the chancel step, remained fixed on his

knees, facing the east, his hat beside him, his hands joined, and he quite unconscious of his appearance in their regard.

When his thanksgiving had come to an end, he arose; the people arose also, and all went out of church together. As soon as the sailor emerged, so that the remaining daylight fell upon his face, old inhabitants began to recognize him as no other than Shadrach Jolliffe, a young man who had not been seen at Havenpool for several years. A son of the town, his parents had died when he was quite young, on which account he had early gone to sea, in the Newfoundland trade.

He talked with this and that townsman as he walked, informing them that, since leaving his native place years before, he had become captain and owner of a small coasting-ketch, which had providentially been saved from the gale as well as himself. Presently he drew near to two girls who were going out of the churchyard in front of him; they had been sitting in the nave at his entry, and had watched his doings with deep interest, afterwards discussing him as they moved out of church together. One was a slight and gentle creature, the other a tall, large-framed, deliberative girl. Captain Jolliffe regarded the loose curls of their hair, their backs and shoulders, down to their heels, for some time.

"Who may those two maids be?" he whispered to his neighbour.

"The little one is Emily Hanning; the tall one Joanna Phippard."

"Ah! I recollect 'em now, to be sure."

He advanced to their elbow, and genially stole a gaze at them.

"Emily, you don't know me?" said the sailor, turning his beaming brown eyes on her.

"I think I do, Mr Jolliffe," said Emily, shyly.

The other girl looked straight at him with her dark eyes.

"The face of Miss Joanna I don't call to

"HE ADVANCED TO THEIR ELBOW, GENIALLY STOLE A GAZE AT THEM, AND SAID, 'EMILY, YOU DON'T KNOW ME?'"

mind so well," he continued. "But I know her beginnings and kindred."

They walked and talked together, Jolliffe narrating particulars of his late narrow escape, till they reached the corner of Sloop Lane, in which Emily Hanning dwelt, when, with a nod and smile, she left them. Soon the sailor parted also from Joanna, and, having no especial errand or appointment, turned back towards Emily's house. She lived with her father, who called himself an accountant, the daughter, however, keeping a little stationery shop as a supplemental provision for the gaps of his somewhat uncertain business. On entering Jolliffe found father and daughter about to begin tea.

"Oh, I didn't know it was teatime," he said. "Ay, I'll have a cup with much pleasure."

He remained to tea and long afterwards, telling more tales of his seafaring life. Several neighbours called to listen, and were asked to come in. Somehow Emily Hanning lost her heart to the sailor that Sunday night,

and in the course of a week or two there was
a tender understanding between them.

One moonlight evening in the next month
Shadrach was ascending out of the town by
the long straight road eastward, to an elevated
suburb where the more fashionable houses
stood—if anything near this ancient port could
be called fashionable—when he saw a figure
before him whom, from her manner of glancing
back, he took to be Emily. But, on coming
up, he found she was Joanna Phippard. He
gave a gallant greeting, and walked beside her.

"Go along," she said, "or Emily will be
jealous!"

He seemed not to like the suggestion, and
remained.

What was said and what was done on that
walk never could be clearly recollected by
Shadrach; but in some way or other Joanna
contrived to wean him away from her gentler
and younger rival. From that week onwards,

Jolliffe was seen more and more in the wake of Joanna Phippard and less in the company of Emily; and it was soon rumoured about the quay that old Jolliffe's son, who had come home from sea, was going to be married to the former young woman, to the great disappointment of the latter.

Just after this report had gone about, Joanna dressed herself for a walk one morning, and started for Emily's house in the little cross street. Intelligence of the deep sorrow of her friend on account of the loss of Shadrach had reached her ears also, and her conscience reproached her for winning him away.

Joanna was not altogether satisfied with the sailor. She liked his attentions, and she coveted the dignity of matrimony; but she had never been deeply in love with Jolliffe. For one thing, she was ambitious, and socially his position was hardly so good as her own, while there was always the chance of an attractive woman mating considerably above her. It had long been in her mind that she would not strongly object to give him back again to Emily if her friend felt so very badly about him. To this end she had penned a letter of renunciation to Shadrach, which letter she carried in her hand, intending to post it if personal observation of Emily convinced her that her friend was suffering.

Joanna entered Sloop Lane and stepped down into the stationery shop, which was below the pavement level. Emily's father was never at home at this hour of the day, and it seemed as though Emily was not at home either, for the visitor could make nobody hear. Customers came so seldom hither that a five minutes' absence of the proprietor counted for little. Joanna waited in the little shop, where Emily had tastefully set out—as women can—articles in themselves of slight value, so as to obscure the meagreness of the stock-in-trade; till she saw a figure pausing without the window apparently absorbed in the contemplation of the sixpenny books, packets of paper, and prints hung on a string. It was Captain Shadrach Jolliffe, peering in to ascertain if Emily was there alone. Moved by an impulse of reluctance to meet him in a spot which breathed of Emily, she slipped through the door that communicated with the parlour at the back. Joanna had frequently done so before, for in her friendship with Emily she had the freedom of the house without ceremony.

Jolliffe entered the shop. Through the thin blind which screened the glass partition she could see that he was disappointed at not finding Emily there. He was about to go out again, when her form darkened the doorway, hastening back from some errand. At sight of Jolliffe she started back as if she would have gone out again.

"Don't run away, Emily; don't!" said he. "What can make ye afraid?"

"I'm not afraid, Captain Jolliffe. Only— only I saw you all of a sudden, and—it made me jump." Her voice showed that her heart had jumped even more than the rest of her.

"I just called as I was passing," he said.

"For some paper?" She hastened behind the counter.

"No, no, Emily. Why do ye get behind there? Why not stay by me? You seem to hate me."

"I don't hate you. How can I?"

"Then come out, so that we can talk like Christians."

Emily obeyed with a fitful laugh, till she stood again beside him in the open part of the shop.

"There's a dear," he said.

"You mustn't say that, Captain Jolliffe; because the words belong to somebody else."

" Ah ! I know what you mean. But, Emily, upon my life I didn't know till this morning that you cared one bit about me, or I should not have done as I have done. I have the best of feelings for Joanna, but I know that from the beginning she hasn't cared for me more than in a friendly way ; and I see now the one I ought to have asked to be my wife. You know, Emily, when a man comes home from sea after a long voyage he's as blind as a bat— he can't see who's who in women. They are all alike to him, beautiful creatures, and he takes the first that comes easy, without thinking if she loves him, or if he might not soon love another better than her. From the first I inclined to you most, but you were so backward and shy that I thought you didn't want me to bother 'ee, and so I went to Joanna."

" Don't say any more, Mr. Jolliffe, don't ! " said she, choking. " You are going to marry

Joanna next month, and it is wrong to—
to—— "

"Oh, Emily, my darling!" he cried, and
clasped her little figure in his arms before she
was aware.

Joanna, behind the curtain, turned pale,
tried to withdraw her eyes, but could not.

"It is only you I love as a man ought to
love the woman he is going to marry; and I
know this from what Joanna has said, that she
will willingly let me off. She wants to marry
higher, I know, and only said 'Yes' to me out
of kindness. A fine, tall girl like her isn't the
sort for a plain sailor's wife; you be the best
suited for that."

He kissed her and kissed her again, her
flexible form quivering in the agitation of his
embrace.

"I wonder—are you sure—Joanna is going
to break off with you? Oh, are you sure?
Because—— "

"I know she would not wish to make us miserable. She will release me."

"Oh, I hope—I hope she will! Don't stay any longer, Captain Jolliffe!"

He lingered, however, till a customer came for a penny stick of sealing-wax, and then he withdrew.

Green envy had overspread Joanna at the scene. She looked about for a way of escape. To get out without Emily's knowledge of her visit was indispensable. She crept from the parlour into the passage, and thence to the front door of the house, where she let herself noiselessly into the street.

The sight of that caress had reversed all her resolutions. She could not let Shadrach go. Reaching home, she burnt the letter, and told her mother that if Captain Jolliffe called she was too unwell to see him.

Shadrach, however, did not call. He sent her a note expressing in simple language the state of his feelings, and asking to be allowed to take advantage of the hints she had given him that her affection, too, was little more than friendly, by cancelling the engagement.

Looking out upon the harbour and the island beyond he waited and waited in his lodgings for an answer that did not come. The suspense grew to be so intolerable that after dark he went up the High Street. He could not resist calling at Joanna's to learn his fate.

Her mother said her daughter was too unwell to see him, and to his questioning admitted that it was in consequence of a letter received from himself, which had distressed her deeply.

" You know what it was about, perhaps, Mrs. Phippard ? " he said.

Mrs. Phippard owned that she did, adding that it put them in a very painful position. Thereupon Shadrach, fearing that he had been guilty of an enormity, explained that if his letter had pained Joanna it must be owing to a misunderstanding, since he had thought it would be a relief to her. If otherwise, he would hold himself bound by his word, and she was to think of the letter as never having been written.

Next morning he received an oral message from the young woman, asking him to fetch her home from a meeting that evening. This he did, and while walking from the Town Hall to her door, with her hand in his arm, she said—

"It is all the same as before between us, isn't it, Shadrach? Your letter was sent in mistake?"

"It is all the same as before," he answered, "if you say it must be."

"I wish it to be," she murmured, with hard lineaments, as she thought of Emily.

Shadrach was a religious and scrupulous man, who respected his word as his life. Shortly afterwards the wedding took place, Jolliffe

8

having conveyed to Emily as gently as possible
the error he had fallen into when estimating
Joanna's mood as one of indifference.

II.

A MONTH after the marriage Joanna's mother
died, and the couple were obliged to turn their
attention to very practical matters. Now that
she was left without a parent, Joanna could
not bear the notion of her husband going to
sea again, but the question was, What could
he do at home? They finally decided to take
on a grocer's shop in High Street, the goodwill
and stock of which were waiting to be disposed
of at that time. Shadrach knew nothing of
shopkeeping, and Joanna very little, but they
hoped to learn.

To the management of this grocery business
they now devoted all their energies, and continued to conduct it for many succeeding years,

without great success. Two sons were born
to them, whom their mother loved to idolatry,
although she had never passionately loved
her husband ; and she lavished upon them all
her forethought and care. But the shop did
not thrive, and the large dreams she had
entertained of her sons' education and career
became attenuated in the face of realities.
Their schooling was of the plainest, but, being
by the sea, they grew alert in all such nautical
arts and enterprises as were attractive to their
age.

The great interest of the Jolliffes' married
life, outside their own immediate household,
had lain in the marriage of Emily. By one
of those odd chances which lead those that lurk
in unexpected corners to be discovered while
the obvious are passed by, the gentle girl had
been seen and loved by a thriving merchant
of the town, a widower, some years older than
herself, though still in the prime of life. At

first Emily had declared that she never, never could marry any one; but Mr. Lester had quietly persevered, and had at last won her reluctant assent. Two children also were the fruits of this union, and, as they grew and prospered, Emily declared that she had never supposed she could live to be so happy.

The worthy merchant's home, one of those large, substantial brick mansions frequently jammed up in old-fashioned towns, faced directly on the High Street, nearly opposite to the grocery shop of the Jolliffes, and it now became the pain of Joanna to behold the woman, whose place she had usurped out of pure covetousness, looking down from her position of comparative wealth upon the humble shop-window with its dusty sugar-loaves, heaps of raisins, and canisters of tea, over which it was her own lot to preside. The business having so dwindled, Joanna was obliged to serve in the shop herself, and it galled and mortified her that Emily

Lester, sitting in her large drawing-room over the way, could witness her own dancings up and down behind the counter at the beck and call of wretched twopenny customers, whose patronage she was driven to welcome gladly : persons to whom she was compelled to be civil in the street, while Emily was bounding along with her children and her governess, and conversing with the genteelest people of the town and neighbourhood. This was what she had gained by not letting Shadrach Jolliffe, whom she had so faintly loved, carry his affection elsewhere.

Shadrach was a good and honest man, and he had been faithful to her in heart and in deed. Time had clipped the wings of his love for Emily in his devotion to the mother of his boys : he had quite lived down that impulsive earlier fancy, and Emily had become in his regard nothing more than a friend. It was the same with Emily's feelings for him.

Possibly, had she found the least cause for
jealousy, Joanna would almost have been better
satisfied. It was in the absolute acquiescence
of Emily and Shadrach in the results she herself had contrived that her discontent found
nourishment.

Shadrach was not endowed with the narrow
shrewdness necessary for developing a retail
business in the face of many competitors. Did
a customer inquire if the grocer could really
recommend the wondrous substitute for eggs
which a persevering bagman had forced into
his stock, he would answer that "when you did
not put eggs into a pudding it was difficult
to taste them there;" and when he was asked
if his "real Mocha coffee" was real Mocha,
he would say grimly, "as understood in small
shops."

One summer day, when the big brick house
opposite was reflecting the oppressive sun's
heat into the shop, and nobody was present

but husband and wife, Joanna looked across at Emily's door, where a carriage had drawn up. Traces of patronage had been visible in Emily's manner of late.

"Shadrach, the truth is, you are not a business man," his wife sadly murmured. "You were not brought up to shopkeeping, and it is impossible for a man to make a fortune at an occupation he has jumped into, as you did into this."

Jolliffe agreed with her, in this as in everything else. "Not that I care a rope's end about making a fortune," he said cheerfully. "I am happy enough, and we can rub on somehow."

She looked again at the great house through the screen of bottled pickles.

"Rub on—yes," she said bitterly. "But see how well off Emmy Lester is, who used to be so poor! Her boys will go to college, no doubt; and think of yours—obliged to go to the National School!"

Shadrach's thoughts had flown to Emily.

"Nobody," he said, good humouredly, "ever did Emily a better turn than you did, Joanna, when you warned her off me and put an end to that little simpering nonsense between us, so as to leave it in her power to say: 'Aye' to Lester when he came along."

This almost maddened her.

"Don't speak of bygones!" she implored, in stern sadness. "But think, for the boys' and my sake, if not for your own, what are we to do to get richer?"

"Well," he said, becoming serious, "to tell the truth, I have always felt myself unfit for this business, though I've never liked to say so. I seem to want more room for sprawling; a more open space to strike out in than here among friends and neighbours. I could get rich as well as any man, if I tried my own way."

"I wish you would! What is your way?"

" To go to sea again."

She had been the very one to keep him at home, hating the semi-widowed existence of sailors' wives. But her ambition checked her instincts now, and she said—

" Do you think success really lies that way ? "

" I am sure it lies in no other."

" Do you want to go, Shadrach ? "

" Not for the pleasure of it, I can tell 'ee. There's no such pleasure at sea, Joanna, as I can find in my back parlour here. To speak honest, I have no love for the brine. I never had much. But if it comes to a question of a fortune for you and the lads, it is another thing. That's the only way to it for one born and bred a seafarer as I."

" Would it take long to earn ? "

" Well, that depends ; perhaps not."

The next morning Shadrach pulled from a chest of drawers the nautical jacket he had

worn during the first months of his return,
brushed out the moths, donned it, and walked
down to the quay. The port still did a fair
business in the Newfoundland trade, though
not so much as formerly.

It was not long after this that he invested all
he possessed in purchasing a part-ownership in
a brig, of which he was appointed captain.
A few months were passed in coast-trading,
during which interval Shadrach wore off the
land-rust that had accumulated upon him in
his grocery phase; and in the spring the brig
sailed for Newfoundland.

Joanna lived on at home with her sons, who
were now growing up into strong lads, and
occupying themselves in various ways about
the harbour and quay.

" Never mind, let them work a little," their
fond mother said to herself. " Our necessities
compel it now, but when Shadrach comes home
they will be only seventeen and eighteen, and

they shall be removed from the port, and their education thoroughly taken in hand by a tutor; and with the money they'll have they will perhaps be as near to gentlemen as Emmy Lester's precious two, with their algebra and their Latin."

The date for Shadrach's return drew near and arrived, and he did not appear. Joanna was assured that there was no cause for anxiety, sailing-ships being so uncertain in their coming; which assurance proved to be well-grounded, for late one wet evening, about a month after the calculated time, the ship was announced as at hand, and presently the slip-slop step of Shadrach as the sailor sounded in the passage, and he entered. The boys had gone out and had missed him, and Joanna was sitting alone.

As soon as the first emotion of reunion between the couple had passed, Jolliffe explained the delay as owing to a small speculative contract, which had produced good results.

"I was determined not to disappoint 'ee," he said; "and I think you'll own that I haven't."

With this he pulled out an enormous canvas bag, full and rotund as the money-bag of the giant whom Jack slew, untied it, and shook the contents out into her lap as she sat in her low chair by the fire. A mass of guineas (there were guineas on the earth in those days) fell into her lap with a sudden thud, weighing down her gown to the floor.

"There!" said Shadrach, complacently. "I told 'ee, dear, I'd do it; and have I done it or no?"

Somehow her face, after the first excitement of possession, did not retain its glory.

"It is a lot of gold, indeed," she said. "And —is this *all?*"

"All? Why, dear Joanna, do you know you can count to three hundred in that heap? It is a fortune!"

" Yes—yes. A fortune—judged by sea; but judged by land—— "

However, she banished considerations of the money for the nonce. Soon the boys came in, and next Sunday Shadrach returned thanks— this time by the more ordinary channel of the italics in the General Thanksgiving. But a few days after, when the question of investing the money arose, he remarked that she did not seem so satisfied as he had hoped.

" Well, you see, Shadrach," she answered, " *we* count by hundreds; *they* count by thousands " (nodding towards the other side of the street). " They have set up a carriage and pair since you left."

" Oh ! have they ? "

" My dear Shadrach, you don't know how the world moves. However, we'll do the best we can with it. But they are rich, and we are poor still."

The greater part of a year was desultorily

spent.   She moved sadly about the house and shop, and the boys were still occupying themselves in and around the harbour.

"Joanna," he said, one day, "I see by your movements that it is not enough."

"It is not enough," said she.   "My boys will have to live by steering the ships that the Lesters own, and I was once above her!"

Jolliffe was not an argumentative man, and he only murmured that he thought he would take another voyage.   He meditated for several days, and coming home from the quay one afternoon, said suddenly—

"I could do it for 'ee, dear, in one more trip, for certain, if—if—— "

"Do what, Shadrach?"

"Enable 'ee to count by thousands instead of hundreds."

"If what?"

"If I might take the boys."

She turned pale.

" Don't say that, Shadrach," she answered hastily.

" Why ? "

" I don't like to hear it. There's danger at sea. I want them to be something genteel, and no danger to them. I couldn't let them risk their lives at sea. Oh, I couldn't ever, ever ! "

" Very well, dear, it shan't be done."

Next day, after a silence, she asked a question—

" If they were to go with you it would make a great deal of difference, I suppose, to the profit ? "

" 'Twould treble what I should get from the venture single-handed. Under my eye they would be as good as two more of myself."

Later on she said, " Tell me more about this ? "

Well, the boys are almost as clever as master-mariners in handling a craft, upon my life. There isn't a more cranky place in the South Seas than about the sandbanks of this harbour, and they've practised here from their infancy. And they are so steady. I couldn't get their steadiness and their trustworthiness in half a dozen men twice their age."

"And is it *very* dangerous at sea; now, too, there are rumours of war?" she asked uneasily.

"Oh, well, there be risks. Still——"

The idea grew and magnified, and the mother's heart was crushed and stifled by it. Emmy was growing *too* patronizing; it could not be borne. Shadrach's wife could not help nagging him about their comparative poverty. The young men, amiable as their father, when spoken to on the subject of a voyage of enterprise, were quite willing to embark; and though they, like their father, had no great love for the sea, they became quite enthusiastic when the proposal was detailed.

Everything now hung upon their mother's assent. She withheld it long, but at last gave the word : the young men might accompany their father. Shadrach was unusually cheerful about it : Heaven had preserved him hitherto, and he had uttered his thanks. God would not forsake those who were faithful to Him.

All that the Jolliffes possessed in the world was put into the enterprise. The grocery stock was pared down to the least that possibly could afford a bare sustenance to Joanna during the absence, which was to last through the usual Newf'nland spell." How she would endure the weary time she hardly knew, for the boys had been with her formerly; but she nerved herself for the trial.

The ship was laden with boots and shoes, ready-made clothing, fishing-tackle, butter, cheese, cordage, sailcloth, and many other commodities; and was to bring back oil, furs, skins, fish, cranberries, and what else came to

9¹

hand. But much trading to other ports was to be undertaken between the voyages out and homeward, and thereby much money made.

III.

THE brig sailed on a Monday morning in spring; but Joanna did not witness its departure. She could not bear the sight that she had been the means of bringing about. Knowing this, her husband told her overnight that they were to sail some time before noon next day; hence when, awakening at five the next morning, she heard them bustling about downstairs, she did not hasten to descend, but lay trying to nerve herself for the parting, imagining they would leave about nine, as her husband had done on his previous voyage. When she did descend she beheld words chalked upon the sloping face of the bureau; but no

husband or sons. In the hastily scrawled lines
Shadrach said they had gone off thus not to
pain her by a leave-taking; and the sons had
chalked under, " Good-bye, mother."

She rushed to the quay, and looked down the
harbour towards the blue rim of the sea, but
she could only see the masts and bulging sails
of the *Joanna;* no human figures. " 'Tis I
have sent them!" she said wildly, and burst
into tears. In the house the chalked Good-
byes nearly broke her heart. But when she
had re-entered the front room, and looked
across at Emily's, a gleam of triumph lit her
thin face at her anticipated release from the
thraldom of subservience.

To do Emily Lester justice, her assumption
of superiority was mainly a figment of Joanna's
brain. That the circumstances of the merchant's wife were more luxurious than Joanna's,
the former could not conceal; though when-
ever the two met, which was not very often

now, Emily endeavoured to subdue the difference by every means in her power.

The first summer lapsed away; and Joanna meagrely maintained herself by the shop, which now consisted of little more than a window and a counter. Emily was, in truth, her only large customer; and Mrs. Lester's kindly readiness to buy anything and everything without questioning the quality had a sting of bitterness in it, for it was the uncritical attitude of a patron, and almost of a donor. The long dreary winter moved on; the face of the bureau had been turned to the wall to protect the chalked words of farewell, for she could never bring herself to rub them out; and she often glanced at them with wet eyes. Emily's handsome boys came home for the Christmas holidays; and still Joanna subsisted as it were with held breath, like a person submerged. Only one summer more, and the spell would end. Towards the end of the time Emily called on

her quondam friend. She had heard that
Joanna began to feel anxious; she had received
no letter from husband or sons for some months.
Emily's silks rustled arrogantly when, in response to Joanna's almost dumb invitation, she
squeezed through the opening of the counter
and into the parlour behind the shop.

"You are all success, and I am all the other
way!" said Joanna.

"But why do you think so?" said Emily.
"They are to bring back a fortune, I hear."

"Ah, will they come? The doubt is more
than a woman can bear. All three in one
ship—think of that! And I have not heard
of them for months!"

"But the time is not up. You should not
meet misfortune half-way."

"Nothing will repay me for the grief of
their absence!"

"Then why did you let them go? You
were doing fairly well."

" I *made* them go ! " she said, turning vehe-
mently upon Emily. " And I'll tell you why !
I could not bear that we should be only
muddling on, and you so rich and thriving.
Now I have told you, and you may hate me
if you will ! "

" I shall never hate you, Joanna."

And she proved the truth of her words afterwards. The end of the autumn came, and the
brig should have been in port; but nothing
like the *Joanna* appeared in the channel between
the sands. It was now really time to be uneasy.
Joanna Jolliffe sat by the fire, and every gust
of wind caused her a cold thrill. She had
always feared and detested the sea; to her it
was a treacherous, restless, slimy creature,
glorying in the griefs of women. " Still," she
said, " they *must* come ! "

She recalled to her mind that Shadrach had
said before starting that if they returned safe
and sound, with success crowning their enter-

prise, he would go as he had gone after his shipwreck, and kneel with his sons in the church, and offer sincere thanks for their deliverance. She went to church regularly morning and afternoon, and sat in the most forward pew, nearest the chancel-step. Her eyes were mostly fixed on that step, where Shadrach had knelt in the bloom of his young manhood : she knew to an inch the spot which his knees had pressed twenty winters before ; his outline as he had knelt, his hat on the step beside him. God was good. Surely her husband must kneel there again : a son on each side as he had said ; George just here, Jim just there. By long watching the spot as she worshipped, it became as if she saw the three returned ones there kneeling ; the two slim outlines of her boys, the more bulky form between them ; their hands clasped, their heads shaped against the eastern wall. The fancy grew almost to an hallucination ; she could

never turn her worn eyes to the step without
seeing them there.

Nevertheless they did not come. Heaven
was merciful, but it was not yet pleased to
relieve her soul. This was her purgation for
the sin of making them the slaves of her
ambition. But it became more than purgation
soon, and her mood approached despair. Months
had passed since the brig had been due, but it
had not returned.

Joanna was always hearing or seeing evidences of their arrival. When on the hill
behind the port, whence a view of the open
Channel could be obtained, she felt sure that a
little speck on the horizon, breaking the eter-
nally level waste of waters southward, was the
truck of the *Joanna's* mainmast. Or when
indoors, a shout or excitement of any kind at
the corner of the Town Cellar, where the High
Street joined the Quay, caused her to spring
to her feet and cry: " 'Tis they ! "

" WHEN ON THE HILL BEHIND THE PORT, WHENCE A VIEW OF THE CHANNEL
COULD BE OBTAINED, SHE FELT SURE THAT A LITTLE SPECK ON THE
HORIZON WAS THE TRUCK OF THE JOANNA'S MAINMAST."

But it was not. The visionary forms knelt every Sunday afternoon on the chancel step, but not the real. Her shop had, as it were, eaten itself hollow. In the apathy which had resulted from her loneliness and grief she had ceased to take in the smallest supplies, and thus had sent away her last customer.

In this strait Emily Lester tried by every means in her power to aid the afflicted woman; but she met with constant repulses.

"I don't like you! I can't bear to see you!" Joanna would whisper hoarsely when Emily came to her and made advances.

"But I want to help and soothe you, Joanna," Emily would say.

"You are a lady, with a rich husband and fine sons. What can you want with a bereaved crone like me?"

"Joanna, I want this: I want you to come and live in my house, and not stay alone in this dismal place any longer."

"And suppose they come and don't find me at home? You wish to separate me and mine! No, I'll stay here. I don't like you, and I can't thank you, whatever kindness you do me."

However, as time went on, Joanna could not afford to pay the rent of the shop and house without an income. She was assured that all hope of the return of Shadrach and his sons was vain, and she reluctantly consented to accept the asylum of the Lesters' house. Here she was allotted a room of her own on the second floor, and went and came as she chose, without contact with the family. Her hair greyed and whitened, deep lines channelled her forehead, and her form grew gaunt and stooping. But she still expected the lost ones, and when she met Emily on the staircase she would say morosely, "I know why you've got me here! They'll come, and be disappointed at not finding me at home, and perhaps go away again; and then you'll be revenged for my taking Shadrach away from 'ee."

Emily Lester bore these reproaches from the grief-stricken soul. She was sure—all the people of Havenpool were sure—that Shadrach and his sons could not return. For years the vessel had been given up as lost. Nevertheless, when awakened at night by any noise, Joanna would rise from bed and glance at the shop opposite by the light from the flickering lamp, to make sure it was not they.

It was a damp and dark December night, six years after the departure of the brig *Joanna*. The wind was from the sea, and brought up a fishy mist which mopped the face like moist flannel. Joanna had prayed her usual prayer for the absent ones with more fervour and confidence than she had felt for months, and had fallen asleep about eleven. It must have been between one and two when she suddenly started up. She had certainly heard steps in the

street, and the voices of Shadrach and her sons
calling at the door of the grocery shop. She
sprang out of bed, and, hardly knowing what
clothing she dragged on herself, hastened down
Emily's large and carpeted staircase, put the
candle on the hall-table, unfastened the bolts
and chain, and stepped into the street. The
mist, blowing up the street from the Quay,
hindered her seeing the shop, although it was
so near; but she had crossed to it in a moment.
How was it? Nobody stood there. The
wretched woman walked wildly up and down
with her bare feet—there was not a soul. She
returned and knocked with all her might at the
door which had once been her own—they might
have been admitted for the night, unwilling to
disturb her till the morning. It was not till
several minutes had elapsed that the young
man who now kept the shop looked out of an
upper window, and saw the skeleton of something human standing below half dressed.

" Has anybody arrived ?" asked the form.

" Oh, Mrs. Jolliffe, I didn't know it was you," said the young man, kindly, for he was aware how her baseless expectations moved her. " No ; nobody has come."

THE GHOST OF THE PAST.

By Mrs. E. LYNN LINTON.

MRS. E. LYNN LINTON.

WE all have our times of supremest bliss—our days of intensest brilliancy. They may be as short-lived as a morning glory, or they may last as long as a summer garden, but there they are— times when we are absolutely content—when we see no clouds on the horizon and forget the storms that lie behind us—days when the flaming sword is sheathed and the Gates of Eden stand open, and we walk through the meadows of asphodel and ama-

ranth, believing in their everlasting beauty,
peace, and fragrance. The glory of fulfilled
ambition makes this time for some, and Honour
clothes the sky with stars that dazzle as they
shine; but Love, dear Love, is the sun itself
and gives us the sweetest and most exquisite of
all our joys. Love, dear Love! what can equal
it for the soul's delight! It combines in itself
all the lustrous hues of life; it is the chord
wherein sound all its loveliest harmonies. It
transforms poverty to wealth; and it builds
that divine City of Enchantment where the
queen is always fair and the prince is always
young. It is the gladdest minister, if also the
cruellest master of man. When we love and
are beloved, we sit with the gods on the hill
of Heaven; when we love and are not beloved,
through change, satiety, or death, we are cast
down into hell with Lucifer and the fallen
angels. Meantime, while we are young—while
the sun shines and the heart beats high and

kisses are still fresh to the lips—while the
roses are in bud and before the silver streaks
the gold—the gods are our friends and earth
is our Paradise. We love and are beloved;
and there is no death nor sorrow in the world!

Had his sensations been put into form
Hubert Gainsborough would have seen something like this written on the sands over which
the tide was swiftly flowing—washing away
those intertwined initials which he had just
drawn on the level beach. He knew that this
was their golden hour, and that he and Naomi
would never be more blessed than they were
now, no, not even when the final sacrament
had separated them from the world and given
them to each other for that wonderful moon
which love makes of honey, and all that is not
love turns to gall. Everything was in their
favour, and their coming marriage was one in
which the most critical, the most censorious,

could find no flaw. It was as smooth as satin
and clear as crystal. Fortune, station, health,
ages—not a crooked straw was on their path—
not a leaf of nightshade presaged the coming
of the deadly witch of misfortune. Naomi had
had no other fancy by which to compare her
lover to his disadvantage, and Hubert had
buried out of sight all his. He had sown his
wild oats and the sack was now empty. And
yet—the harvest? Bitter enough at the time,
was it really all stacked and garnered? Might
not some aftermath crop up again when least
expected? The passover is vitiated for the
pious Jew if but one measure of leaven remains.
What of the passover of the Fates who pursue,
of the Vengeance which strikes, if aught of
that bitter harvest of youthful folly remains?

Why did the thought of her suddenly cross
his mind at this moment? Why did Naomi's
bended neck make him slightly shiver as if a
cold wind had passed over him, gorgeous,

10

burning summer time as it was? As she stooped her head, looking into the little pool where the sea-flowers had s｜read out their coloured rays, the sunlight caught the fringe at the back of her neck, and the brown of her hair was brightened into gold.

A sudden longing to kiss those feathery little curls flushed him like a fever; and then a thought checked his impulse and made his blood run cold as if a wandering ghost had touched him as it passed. The last time he kissed a woman's neck, there at the back, he had been sitting, as now, on the sands of the seashore. But it had been in France—at that glaring, garish Trouville—not in a leafy little home-bay in Devonshire; and, instead of Naomi Ponsonby, pledged to be his wife before the year was out, his companion had been the beautiful American, Mariquita Delmare, with whom there had never been a question of marriage. For was not that burly, black-

bearded, crop-haired man who, once a week,
came down to see her, and of whom she was
evidently so much afraid, Auguste Delmare
and her husband? All the same, wife as
she was—or seemed to be—Hubert had loved
this woman with the intensity of a young
man's first serious passion. And when his
enlightenment came, nothing but the anger of
contempt had saved him from the heartbreak
of despair.

But why should he think of her now? As
things had shaped themselves in his life it was
a kind of sacrilege to remember her at all.
To be actively reminded of her by Naomi was
blasphemous.

Naomi saw the change in her lover's face—
it was as if a cloud had come over the sun.
Not being a woman of obtrusive sympathy nor
of inquisitive affection, instead of speaking or
asking why, she laid her hand on his with a
caressing touch that told all she wished to say.

It was such a gentle, tender little touch!—so womanly in its sympathy, but yet so almost childish in its ignorance of the reason why! It was to Hubert what the harp of David was to Saul. The cloud passed—the wandering ghost vanished. Mariquita Delmare faded into the void of nothingness; and all that Hubert saw was Naomi Ponsonby sitting there in the sunlight beside him—the angel whom the gods had given to bless and beautify his life—the divine maiden so soon to become his dear wife!

He took her hand and kissed it. What a beautiful hand it was! Those long taper fingers and that generous palm expressed her character in its mixture of idealistic morality and human tenderness. By the one she held a lofty standard and would be an inflexible judge; by the other she opened her arms to the suffering, and banished from her heart no one whom that heart could succour.

" The loveliest hand in the whole world !"

said Hubert, tracing the veins and outlining the fingers after he had kissed it as a saint might kiss a relic; but also as a lover kisses the hand of the beloved.

"Said by the most unblushing flatterer in the whole world!" laughed Naomi.

"Love cannot flatter," he answered, looking at her with eyes as full of admiration as those roses at her throat were full of colour and perfume.

"I think it does nothing else," she returned, still laughing.

She was so happy that everything made her laugh. Like a child, the whole earth seemed to be one great throb of joy.

"Then all you say to me is flattery, hey?" said Hubert. "Ah, sweet, my sweet, you have put yourself into a cleft stick! How will you get out of it?"

"But I never do flatter you as you flatter me," she said. "When did I tell you that this thing about you was so beautiful, and that so charming? Never!"

"If you have not in so many words, you have twenty times by those great grey eyes of yours!" he answered with mock self-complacency. "I know you admire me immensely, and think me no end of a fine fellow; so we are quits after all—only I am the most candid."

"I do not agree to that—not the least in the world," she cried with commendable energy.

Again Hubert's face changed. Why was he so sensitive to-day? The fun passed out of it for pain to take its place.

"What! you do not love me as much as I love you?" he said in a disturbed voice. "You tell me that seriously, Naomi?"

She turned to him with a mocking little mouth and mischievous arched brows, meaning to carry on the play. Lovers find nothing too silly as the medium of verbal caressing; and silly as was this little interlude, it served its purpose. But her mocking smile and saucy answer died on her lips. There was something in her lover's face not to be met by a joke.

" Love you, Hubert?—as much as you love me ? " she repeated. " Do you need to ask ? " Then with a sudden blush and the sweetest, loveliest air of self-surrender, she added—both her hands now on one of his : " Yes, I do love you as much as you love me. If love could be weighed, as we weighed the honeycomb yesterday, perhaps mine would be the most ! "

" That is impossible, Naomi," he answered gravely. " You might as well say you could add to infinity or lengthen eternity ! " He put his disengaged arm round her and drew her to him. " My darling, my own darling," he said, all his heart in his voice ; " I love you as I never loved living woman before."

Naomi caught at the words. That black drop which we all have in our hearts under different names and shapes was in hers a certain form of jealousy,—the jealousy, the exactingness, of a pure and inexperienced woman demanding as much as she gave.

"Then you have loved before?" she said a little coldly, instinctively taking away her hands.

"Not as I love you," he answered, trying to cover his mistake by extra fervour. "I love you as no man ever loved since the world began! You do not know what I feel for you, Naomi. You are like God and heaven to me! You are my good angel: and God gave you to me! I love you, darling, almost more than a man should—more than is well for my peace."

His passion gained her. What woman could have resisted?

"Give me your peace, I will take care of it," she said with infinite tenderness. "If we love each other, Hubert, no harm can come to us. Nothing but death can separate us, and even that will not divide us."

"Nothing but death? You swear that?" he said. "Only death will separate us, Naomi, and even that will not divide us?"

"Yes," she answered solemnly; "I swear it."

"Without reservation?"

"What reservation should I have?" she returned, with an incredulous little smile. "The only reservation would be if you had loved any one else as you love me, or had done anything wrong; and that is too absurd to imagine!"

She looked at him with her soft grey eyes as full of womanly love as his had been of the man's stronger passion. He was right. Those eyes expressed her admiration of him as plainly as if her lips had uttered all that was in her heart of praise and hymn to his honour. To her he was the perfect man—flawless, faultless —and she was not ashamed to show what she would not have dared to say.

The remembrance of that past sin flowed like the salt waters of tears over his head. Like a spectre Mariquita Delmare again seemed to float before him, filling the whole air with her baleful beauty; but for his best exorcism he looked again into Naomi's upturned face, and soothed himself with that futile anodyne: "She will never know !"

The tie between these two young people had in it something more than love, for Hubert, at the risk of his own life, had saved that of Geoffrey Ponsonby, Naomi's only brother ; and thus the acquaintance which then began was founded on the deepest feelings of our human nature. To the Ponsonbys Hubert was an incarnation of divine power to whom they owed anew that beloved life so nearly lost; while to him they had the claim which conferring a benefit establishes on him who confers it. They gave him the devotion of gratitude, but he gave them the even stronger feeling of

responsibility. The life he had saved he felt
in some measure belonged to him to care
for; and as he was eight years older than
Geoffrey—thirty to the younger man's two
and twenty—he took his obligation seriously,
and was like the boy's elder brother, even
before his engagement with Naomi gave him
the additional right of future relationship.

All things come to an end, and this lovely
idyl had to end with the rest. The westering
sun brought with its slanting rays the prosaic
claims of dinner and domestic life generally;
and the young people had nothing for it but
to go back to Ivy Lodge, and do the best they
could with the verandah and the moonlight,
against the background of the lighted room
where gentle Mrs. Ponsonby played Patience
by herself, and thought of the time when she
too had sat out in the summer moonlight with
her beloved, as happy as Naomi was now.

As they came to the house they were met at

the door by Mrs. Ponsonby in a state of unusual excitement.

"What is it, mother?" asked Naomi, who had that double sense which is given by keen perceptions.

"I have had a letter from Geoff," said Mrs. Ponsonby, a little breathlessly.

"Well?—what?—what does he say?" asked Hubert.

"Such a foolish boy!—so foolish and so wrong! He has engaged himself to a lady whom he confesses to be older than himself, and a widow too. It is madness!"

"Who is she?" again asked Hubert.

"An American," was the answer.

"What American?" he asked quickly. He shivered slightly, as once before to-day on the sands.

"A Mrs. Marillier," was the answer.

Hubert drew a deep breath, and the blood came back into his face.

" Geoffrey says she is wonderfully beautiful," the mother went on to say ; " and as good as she is lovely. She is very well connected— belongs to an old Virginian family—and has money of her own, so that, as he says, she does not take him for his. At all events there it is ; and now what am I to do ? I cannot allow it to go on," she added, woman-like answering her own question ; " but what am I to do ? "

" Opposition to a thing of this kind does not do much good," said Hubert. " Men have to wear through their own experiences."

" But he is not a man—he is only a boy ! " cried Mrs. Ponsonby. " He has had no ex- perience of life, beyond that to be had at Cambridge, which cannot be much. He is not accustomed yet to the management of the estate—and the idea of an engagement at his age, and with a widow older than himself, is preposterous ! It cannot be allowed. I will not allow it ! "

" If he loves her, my dear, he will not break with her, even though a mother disapproves," said Hubert. " Why should he ? That is the first thing he will say to himself. If he has committed himself and gained her affections he is so far bound to her by honour; and if she has money and all that, and is of known rank and parentage, and there is nothing against her, why should he break with her because he is only twenty-two ? That is a fault which cures itself every day ! You see we must look at it from his point of view, not only our own. To you and to us all it may be foolish and premature; but to him it is the sublimest wisdom and an honourable engagement."

" Then do you advise me to countenance such criminal absurdity ? " said Mrs. Ponsonby, hotly.

" For the present, in a fashion, sprinkling a little cold water judiciously, and not going in for a shower bath," he answered. " A boy of

Geoff's age wants more careful guidance than a man. He has to be led very gently—very tenderly—and the thread must be of silk and invisible!"

"That is so true!" said Naomi, to whom Hubert was incarnate wisdom.

She would have said the same, however, had he advocated strenuous opposition and parental coercion; so that her opinion was not of much value.

But Mrs. Ponsonby still fumed, and the only ray of comfort that she could find in the present distressful moment was when Hubert promised to write very seriously to her boy, and to begin that process of judicious sprinkling which he advised her to adopt. But, above all, he was to find out everything there was to know about this Mrs. Marillier — this beautiful American with money—this widow, a little older than the unmatured and well-endowed young man she had condescended to accept as her future husband. With which promise the poor woman was forced to be content; though, indeed, there was not much content for any one—for after this question of Geoffrey and his fascinating widow had been so far arranged, and Hubert had time to look at his own letters, he found one from his lawyer which cut short his stay at Ivy Lodge, and sent him back at once to Cumberland, where his place was. It was a letter which admitted of no denial, and of business which admitted of no delay. He must pack up to-night and be off by the first train to-morrow morning—those sweet idyls on the sands rudely and roughly interrupted, and his beloved left to the cold keeping of resignation.

All lovers' partings are sad, and their melancholy forebodings are as universal as the tears which express, and the kisses which seem rather to confirm than to banish them. It was to Naomi, and to Hubert too, as if their sun

had set for ever. There was no more daylight
for them, and no more summer. The chill of
death had fallen on their happiness; for at the
best their letters would be only a kind of
twilight—only the autumn flush for the summer
glory. But it had to be done, and he must go.
The time of probation would soon be over now.
This was August, and they would be married
in October. Two months—an eternity to the
separated and impatient young, but to the more
accurate reckoners of time a mere nothing. So
they tried to comfort each other as with trembling voices and pale lips they bade each other
farewell and said :

"It will not be for long!"

Geoffrey's answer to the coldly cautious
letter of his mother was characteristic of his
boyish love. To her diplomacy he opposed the
impetuosity of a first passion and the blindness
of unlimited trust. His eyes were filled with

11

but the one light; and like a newly-converted zealot he was anxious that she should share in the grace he had gained. Without giving time for denial, he announced his arrival with his future bride that very evening. To see her was to love her, he said; and the best excuse he could offer for what might seem his rash-ness in engaging himself at his age was— herself. Wherefore his mother and Naomi must expect them that evening; and he knew that in this visit, hurried and unceremonious as it was, he had done the best thing for them and for her, and that they would congratulate him on his good fortune in securing the most beautiful and the noblest woman on the face of the earth.

No answer could be given to this letter; and to telegraph a refusal that should meet them midway and turn them back on their journey was not quite like gentle Mrs. Ponsonby, whose worst moods were merely fretfulness, never

rising into anger nor deepening into sullenness.
Thus mother and sister had nothing for it but
to make the best of things as they were, and to
hope that this new woman was really the
phœnix Geoffrey's love had painted her.

So far he had calculated rightly. When
Mrs. Ponsonby and Naomi came face to face
with this fair marvel, they no longer wondered
at the boyish infatuation which had staked so
heavily on love and trust. She was so beautiful! She was so graceful in all her movements, so sweet and tender in her manner, and
yet so bright in speech and intelligence! She
had the loveliest little ways that ever woman
had; she said the most charming things; and
she had the daintiest accent—half French, half
American—that gave her voice, which was
naturally harsh and grating, a kind of caressing
intonation by which its native hardness was
made as lovely as soft music. Her dress was a
dream of art; her face a poem of beauty. She

had bright golden hair—very bright gold—
with dark eyebrows and dark lashes, and the
loveliest complexion of milk and roses. Her
eyes were like stars, quick, glancing, and of
varying expression. Sometimes they were as
holy as a saint's, and sometimes they were
veiled as if with a substance, letting not a
thought, not a feeling show through. But
varied as their expression was, they were
watchful eyes—always watchful; eyes that
seemed to listen as well as see, like those of
men accustomed to danger and dependent for
salvation on their own quickness of apprehen-
sion and clearness of prevision. And the
lashes cast the most curious little rim of black-
ness round the lids; and the red of her lips
was of the clearest and most sharply defined
outline imaginable. No blurring here; no
mingling of red and white through the dis-
figuring medium of tears, nor even through the
blush-rose bruise of kisses! Altogether she

was delightful—splendidly delightful; and the
mother and daughter were fascinated, as
Geoffrey knew they would be—as, years ago,
Christabel was fascinated by the Lady Geraldine.

The small round table at the side was full of
photographs. Side by side with Naomi—
Naomi following the mother and Geoffrey—
was the portrait of Hubert Gainsborough.
Mrs. Marillier looking over the room as
strangers do, came in due time to this table
and the four photographs in one line. She
caught her breath as one suddenly surprised,
and the blood gathered round her heart—
though it did not leave her cheek nor lips
paler than before; but she had the undaunted
spirit of one playing for high stakes, with the
full consciousness of what she risked and what
she might win, and it was a principle with her
to face her dangers on the instant.

"Is that another brother?" she asked quite
naturally, taking the photographs in her hand

as if to examine them critically. " How good they all are!—but I did not know you had an elder brother, Geoffrey. You never told me that. I do not see much likeness, however," she added smilingly to Mrs. Ponsonby. " He is not like you nor Naomi nor my boy."

" I forgot to tell you about him," said Geoffrey. " I have forgotten everything of late! No, that is not a brother—yet; though he is almost more than one. He is the dearest old fellow in the world—Hubert Gainsborough —and he is going to marry Naomi."

" Oh!" said Mrs. Marillier, with a soft smile, turning to her future sister-in-law. " How happy you must be! If he is as lovely a man as mine, and you are as content as I am, you have nothing to complain of!"

" He is very nice, and I am quite happy," said Naomi.

Then they all laughed ; and the rest of the evening passed as such evenings do, on velvet,

where the hours are wreathed with flowers and
Time is shod in gold.

But upstairs in her own room the woman
who called herself Mariquita Marillier had to
face a very different state of things. The
ghost of her bad past had risen up before her
when least expected and most unwelcome ; and
she had to reason out her position, and calcu-
late her chances of escape from the dangers
threatening her like wild beasts prowling
round an open arbour.

"Can I dare it?" she thought; "or shall I
give it all up? Will he have the cruelty, the
dishonour, to betray me? No, he dare not!
His interests are as much at stake as mine.
We are both in the same boat. If I am ship-
wrecked he will be swamped too; for such
ignorant innocents as these will see no difference between us. I can tell my own story, and
it will go hard with me if I do not cut the
ground from under his feet if he is brutal

enough to put a spoke in my wheel. I will brave it, and I will defy him. He used to be fond of me; and men who have once loved a woman as he loved me have always a soft spot left. They are not like us, the fools—and I will take my chance!"

"She is perfectly lovely, and fascinating to an extraordinary degree," Naomi wrote to her lover; "but both mother and I like her so much better when we are with her than when we do not see her. I cannot explain why, nor can mother, but we feel when she is away from us that she is not quite so nice, and we both have to be conquered again. She always does conquer us; that I must confess. It is very odd, but do you not understand what I mean? But she is so clever, and she must be so good! She talks a great deal about God and the Noble Life, and how people have to live for others not themselves, and to walk by the law of the spirit not of the mere intellect. She is, so she

says of herself, a mystic : and I, who am stupid,
do not always understand her. But she is so
sharp and clever! She knows everything—all
we think, and sometimes what we had not
made clear to ourselves till she, as it were,
interpreted our own thoughts. I think she
sees that odd change of feeling in us, for she
said yesterday to mother and me, when we
were walking in the garden : ' The impression
people make and the impression they leave are
sometimes so different ! I have often felt that
living charm of a personality, and then a
certain coldness in absence. But I have always
put the defect down to myself. I think it is
my own failing in sympathy—some note wanting in my own chord of harmony—not any
want or failing in the person. When I am
with these people whom I love in presence and
fall off from in absence, their magnetism supplies my own deficiency and the full chord is
sounded—the notes wanting to me are given

by them.' So perhaps it is mother's and my
own fault, as she seemed to hint; and she is
very charming. She says she is one year
older than Geoff—twenty-three; and she does
not look more, excepting at the end of the
evening, when she gets tired. Then·she looks
thirty and more; and her face quite changes.
If she were not such a pure-hearted noble
creature both mother and I would think she
painted; but we do not like to even imagine
it, because women who paint cannot possibly
be nice—and she is more than nice! Her
husband was a stockbroker in San Francisco;
and she has a pretty Spanish name—Mariquita
—and I believe, but I am not quite sure, that
her maiden name was Delmare."

So now Hubert understood it all. What he
had dimly feared was true, and the woman
whom he knew to be unfit for the companionship of even the ordinarily frail was the
affianced wife of Geoffrey Ponsonby—the boy

for whose life he had made himself in a manner
responsible — the brother of his own future
wife. Mariquita Marillier, the sister-in-law of
Naomi—Mariquita, the woman whom he had
known as the wife of Auguste Delmare! The
ghost of the past had risen up against him—
the after crop was sprouting—and the mills of
God were grinding, not slowly now! This
marriage must be prevented if it broke
Geoffrey's heart and his own. He knew
Naomi's high standard of morality; he knew,
too, the strain of jealousy which lifted up her
love from what else might have been something
like the abjectness of devotion and gave it the
dignity of self-respect. She was utterly
ignorant of life as it is; and she was of the
school which makes no distinction between
men and women. The little that she knew of
vice—all in the clouds as it was—made the
dereliction of the one as shameful as the
abandonment of the other ; and it had not been

Hubert's duty to enlighten her. He therefore knew how she would feel and where he should stand. It would be the overthrowing evidence, and perhaps her love would go with her ideal. She had often said that her love for him was so great because of her respect. Her perfect man as he was—what would it be when she found out how imperfect he had been?—jealous as well as pure; when she learned that he had loved so passionately and sinned so deeply, what would she do? And if even she forgave him—but she would not—would not the bloom of her nature, of her very love, be gone? Would it not be like the violation of her soul, and the acceptance of his sin because she had lost her virginal horror of evil?

Still it had to be done, come what would. He must be so far faithful to that higher law which sacrifices ease and happiness and love itself to duty and the right.

It was impossible to go to Ivy Lodge for the

next day or two, but Hubert wrote to Geoffrey
asking him what he knew of the fascinating
widow, other than by her own report ?—where
he had met her ?—who had vouched for her ?—
what he knew of her past history, her family,
her money itself ? Had he had any corrobora-
tion of her own story, or had he taken everything on trust ? The world was full of these
desultory women, these quasi adventuresses
who thought to efface in a foreign country the
tainted record of their own. He must be quite
sure who it was he was trusting, and who it
was he proposed to give as a daughter to his
mother and a sister to Naomi.

The boy wrote back a fiery letter, as was to
be expected. To have saved his life from
drowning did not entitle Hubert to doubt his
beloved—one of the noblest, purest, most saintly
women that ever lived. If he heard her talk
as she did last night, he would know then what
a priceless treasure he (Geoffrey) had found,

and would blush for his base suspicions. Besides, *he* (Geoffrey) was satisfied, and he was the person most nearly concerned. His marriage was to take place now at once. There was nothing to wait for ; and his mother had consented. She saw the exquisite loveliness, the rare nobility of Mariquita's nature ; and Naomi too loved her. Yet, sweet good girl as Naomi was, she was not equal to Mariquita in sublimity of thought. Hubert would love her too. He must come now at once to Ivy Lodge and join the circle of worshippers. He could not resist ; no one could.

The lad blew off the steam as he wrote, and by the time he ended had got through his anger, and was once more the old, joyous, irresponsible boy-lover who saw no dangers and no difficulties anywhere. He was so happy that he could afford to be magnanimous and to forgive the insult of the doubt.

How well Hubert knew it all ! The false

modesties, the artificial refinement, the high
poetic moralities said beneath the moon—the
lies, deceptions, devilries practised in the face
of day ;—the cleverness which made infamy
look like purity overcome by love, and gave
to the putrescent shimmer of corruption the
glory of God's own sun ! He knew it all, and
understood the net in which she had taken
those dear ones in their quiet Devonshire
home ; for had he not himself once been held
fast even as the boy was held now—as Naomi
and her mother were held ?

They met alone on the sands, where he had
sat with Naomi on that blessed day of summer
only so short a time ago by the passage of the
days, but so long—long as eternity—by the
dating of events.

" I give you your choice," he said. " Leave
the house as you like, secretly or openly—take
your own way of rupture — but break the .

engagement and set the boy free at any cost, or I will break it by telling all I know. In the former way you keep your fair fame here; in the latter you lose it. This marriage has to be cancelled in either case."

"By the first Mr. Hubert Gainsborough escapes scot-free; by the second he suffers with me," said Mariquita, quietly.

"That I know and am prepared for," was Hubert's answer.

"And companionship in misfortune is pleasant," she returned. "If you are really set on this absurd bit of Quixotism you shall smart for it, *mon cher.* I am not disposed to be made the scapegoat, and sent into the wilderness carrying your sins as well as my own. We will go together, Hubert."

"I am ready," said Hubert, sternly.

"To give up Naomi?"

"To give up Naomi that I may save Geoffrey."

She laughed in a mocking kind of way.

"You were not such a tepid lover to me," she said. "I do not think you would have given up *me* for any such high-falutin morality! At least I know that Mr. Delmare—my husband then—and the seventh commandment did not terrify you!"

"I did not give you up till I knew you," said Hubert. "While I believed in you I would have gone down into hell for you. To have died for you would have been easy."

"And I for you," she said, suddenly changing her tone; "for I loved you, Hubert—loved you faithfully—loved you as I never loved before nor have since. I had to deceive you. Bad as I was how could I tell my sad story to a man so young as you were then, with all your illusions unbroken? It would have killed you. I loved you, my darling, and you loved me. Will not the memory of that love soften you? I want only the opportunity to be good. I am

12

not bad at heart—I never was. I have been the victim of a cruel fate and the sport of circumstances, but I was never really vicious. Help me to redeem myself and to make Geoffrey's life blessed, as I can and will make it. He will never know. I will be so good to him! Help me, Hubert, for old times' sake!"

She spoke with inconceivable passion. Her words flowed like a stream of fiery lava; and as she uttered her last appeal she knelt on the sands at his feet and took his hand in both of hers, carrying it to her lips.

Lovely in her passion, graceful in her self-abandonment, with the eloquence of despair in her voice and manner, with the wonderful magnetism of her nature shining in her eyes and drawing out the very heart of her hearer, she was at this moment as dangerous to Hubert's resolve as she had formerly been to his soul. Her appeal was one which touches every true man. To help her to be good!—to help her to

"A BOAT DRIFTED NOISELESSLY ROUND THE HEADLAND, AND NAOMI AND GEOFFREY SPRANG ON SHORE."

redeem herself! — to lift her from the mire where, as she said, a cruel fate had cast her, and where he himself had helped to fling her, and set her cleansed among the shining ranks of the redeemed! If he would not! If for the shadowy idealism of exclusiveness he failed to do the real good laid before him to do!

Genuine tears came into her eyes; her painted lips quivered with a genuine emotion. Hubert put his hand over his eyes. He was trembling like a leaf, for the task was very hard.

" It cannot be !" he said with a sob. " For her sake and his, I must not ! "

A boat drifted noiselessly round the headland, and Naomi and Geoffrey sprang on shore.

" God in Heaven, what does this mean ? " cried Geoffrey, dashing up the beach, to seize Hubert by the throat.

Naomi stood where she was, paralyzed and as if in a dream.

Mariquita started to her feet. She read her doom in Hubert's face, now stern and stiffened as if carved in stone, and she knew that the game was lost.

"I was rehearsing an old play with my former lover, Hubert Gainsborough," she said in her hard, harsh, strident voice;—"the man who seduced me when I was Auguste Delmare's wife."

Years had passed since this bolt fell from the blue and shattered the lives of all concerned. How often the summer had faded into the autumn, and the autumn had died into winter since then, and what tragedies had wrought out their course to the end;—Geoffrey's lifeless body cast up by the tide, how drowned, whether by accident or design, no one ever knew;—the beautiful woman by whom had been wrought all this woe, dead of misery and want, stranded like so much drift wood on

the shores of time and disease;—Naomi and
her mother, like dim spectres of their former
selves, wandering restlessly, aimlessly, joylessly
through the world; Hubert banished like another
Adam from the paradise where he had lived
with Love and walked with God;—all the roses
dead, all the sunlight gone;—what a term of
isolation!—what a blank life was to the three
remaining! The two who had found their rest
in the grave were happier than those who still
lived beneath the sky. Sorrow, shame, futile
despair and as futile repentance—what an after-
crop of that bitter harvest of youthful folly!

"Ought I to have pardoned him?" said
Naomi, often to herself; but Hubert never
asked his heart: "Ought I to have concealed
it?" Cost all it had, it was better than a life
of deception, the white-washing of infamy, and
the association of Naomi and Geoffrey with
the wife of Auguste Delmare—the widow of
Marillier, the stockbroker of San Francisco.

Long parted, they met again one winter moonlight night in the Coliseum at Rome. This place of death and ruin, filled with the memories of love, joy, glory, and martyrdom, all buried deep in the past, it was the fitting place for them to meet. And it was the fitting time—night for day; winter for summer; the pale moon, which threw black fantastic shadows on a ruin, for the glorious sun which had touched all living nature with gold and colour. When they met it was almost as if they too were ghosts with the rest; but that momentary hesitation of each passed like a cloud, and their hands clasped, one the other, too frankly for even the shadow of doubt.

"Shall we never bury our dead, Naomi?" he asked. "Will you never forgive me?—never reinstate me?"

"Not while she lives. She stands between us," said Naomi; but she spoke faintly, and as if with reluctance.

" She is dead," he answered; " only the ghost of the past divides us. Is that as strong as the living present ? "

" Can I ever trust or believe you again ? " she asked sadly.

" If the anguish of all these years gives assurance, yes," he returned. " Oh, Naomi, did you not swear to be always true to me ?— always, always, and through everything ? "

" I have been true," she said. " I have never loved any one else, not for a moment."

" But if you love me ? "

She turned away her head. She did not wish the moonlight to shine on the tears that came into her eyes.

He took her hands and drew them up to his breast, and she did not resist.

" But if you love me ? " he said again, very gently.

She hesitated ;—her heart beating fast, her bosom palpitating. Then suddenly, with the

old sweet action of self-surrender, she turned
to him looking at him with the same eyes of
love as used to look at him in the summer-time
so long ago.

"I have always loved you, Hubert," she
said softly; "and I have never ceased to pray
for you. Perhaps God has heard me and has
given us back to each other as an answer to
my prayers for pardon—pardon for myself as
well as for you. Perhaps I was too hard—will
you accept my repentance?"

REBECCA'S REMORSE.

By JAMES PAYN.

JAMES PAYN.

It is not unusual with young men of philanthropical or religious instincts to seek their work, on taking orders, in the East End of London, and to turn their backs upon fashionable congregations and gift slippers; and yet those "angels of fiction," as they have been termed, the doctors, are never credited with the same self-sacrificing motives. No medical man is ever described as preferring a poor neighbourhood to a rich one; he goes to Bayswater if he

cannot get to Belgravia, and to Bloomsbury if
he cannot get to Bayswater, but further east
than Bloomsbury he is not to be found—in
fiction. This is not in accordance with his
angelic character; with his sending in his little
account receipted to his poor patient; with his
giving him the money for a seaside holiday
instead of a prescription; or with the furnishing
of every comfort for mind and body which that
marvellous diagnosis of his has discerned to be
necessary at the first glance. This is hard, as
there really *are* doctors in the East End of
London, and I once had a practice there myself.

It was not a good one in point of remunera-
tion, and there were plenty of patients; the
sort of " practice " that makes one " perfect "
from a professional point of view; and at the
same time absolves one from the income tax.
I confess, however, that I did not make this
choice of my own free will. " Not grace, nor
zeal," but a quarrel with my respected uncle, on

whom I was entirely dependent, had been the cause of it. I had, I allow, considerably exceeded my allowance at college, and my hospital career in London had been expensive; but his conduct in buying a practice for me in the east instead of the west, as a punishment for, what he did not hesitate to term, my reckless extravagance, was, I think it will be admitted, vindictive. He made me, however, an allowance, which, though one would have called it moderate in a more fashionable locality, was ample enough for such a neighbourhood. Pleasures were very cheap there, and not very attractive. Its concerts were not, at the time of which I am speaking, classical; though of late years music of quite a high class has emigrated thither, and Bethnal Green itself has become an art centre. The dances one was invited to (by advertisement) were of a public nature, and were too much of a maritime character to suit the landsman. There was

no shop where you could spend money to any
extent save that wonderful emporium where
not only lions and tigers are as plentiful as
chickens in Leadenhall Market, but much finer
"curios" are to be found than can be picked
up in Piccadilly.   But lions were not in my
way (though I had kept a "tiger" at the
University), and I was much too young to care
for curios, a taste for which does not usually
develop till the mind has given way a little.

This enforced economy had, however, one
very pleasant side to it; I generally found myself with money in my pocket, a most unusual
experience with an East End doctor.   There is
nothing more distressing to him—if he is a
good fellow, or even if he has a human heart
in his breast—than the knowledge that half
the patients who come under his care are not
so much in need of medicine, as of the neces-
saries of life, with which he is unable to supply
them.   No one knows what poverty is, who

has not seen the East End during a bad time; for my part it was a revelation to me, and when one saw how far, not a shilling, but even a penny was made to go, it gave one a nasty jar to remember the hundreds one had squandered for spending's sake. At first, indeed, brought face to face with such urgent want, one's heart made one lose one's head, and I found myself, not from philanthropy, but from fastidious disgust at squalor and wretchedness, supporting some of the idlest and most worthless scoundrels in the parish; but after a while one grew wiser or less emotional, and learnt discretion, which is the better part of charity. It was a good school for me, in many ways, though I did not like being sent to it.

People talk of "genteel poverty" as being the worst sort of it, but at the risk of being thought material and commonplace, I venture to remark that abject poverty—the halfpennyworth of bread, and the sack instead of a bed

on the floor—is much more hard to bear.
There are degrees even in that, or rather the
same wretchedness seems greater or less, according to the habits of those who endure it.
It is possible, though by no means easy, to be
cleanly under the most sordid conditions; the
house—or rather the one room—may be swept,
though it cannot be garnished; the broken
tea-cup may be washed; the ragged blanket
mended, but when squalor is added to want,
pity is lost in disgust, and the attempt to cling
to the decencies of life is the most touching of
all the attributes of the very poor. It is not,
God help them, often made; when everything
else has gone by the board, it seems useless to
look after the hen-coop.

Star Court, a locality where some of my most
wretched clients dwelt, made very little effort
in this direction, though, as a rule, they were
decent people who dwelt there. We have all
a tendency to live among those of our own

calling—how else (since they are far from loving one another) can the congregation of doctors in Wimpole Street, or lawyers in Bedford Row, be accounted for ?—and when we have no calling, among those of our own taste and habits, and so Star Court had become known in time as a quiet street. New-comers, impecunious as the rest of my colony, but averse to rows and ruffianism, gravitated thither sooner or later ; I used to fancy there were more people who had seen better days there than elsewhere ; but, at all events, they could hardly have seen worse. It was a miserable spot ; but it was not necessary to ask the policeman to keep his eye on you, when you went into Star Court, which was but a reasonable precaution in some other localities.

My first introduction to it was owed to Rebecca Bent, who called upon me one very warm evening in late August to ask for medical advice. I had seen her before, for she had been charwoman for a few weeks at the little house I occupied, when one of my two domestics was away. I remembered her, because she had worked so hard ("like a horse," my cook had said) during that temporary engagement, and given much greater satisfaction than charwomen usually do. Otherwise there was nothing about her to enlist the memory. She was not young—five and forty, one would say, at least, and she had not even the remains of good looks. A tall, big-boned masculine woman, her only claim on the sentimental emotions that look of hopeless discontent worn by so many of her class and age, she was certainly not an attractive person. She was strong enough, however, and to all appearance healthy, and the last person I should have expected to need my professional services. Still, strange as it may seem in the case of those who have so many genuine troubles, it is not more unusual for the very poor to imagine

"WELL, REBECCA, NOTHING GONE WRONG, I HOPE?"

themselves ill, when there is little the matter
with them, than for a fine lady; if they cut
their finger, they think they are like to die.
And the woman had rung the surgery bell,
which (though scarcely in the City sense)
meant business. ·

"Well, Rebecca, nothing gone wrong, I
hope?" I said cheerfully. "You *look* all
right."

"Appearances are deceitful, sir, Heavens
knows," she answered, with what seemed, for so
trite a proverb, a most unnecessary significance.
"It's weakness so that one cannot lift one's
hand to one's head, and thirst so that one wants
a bucketful, and a cough that seems to tear
one's inside out, and besides that there's fever."

"So bad as that, is it?"

I made the usual examination. Her pulse
was all right, her tongue quite a pleasure to
look at, as compared with most of those organs
submitted to my inspection (especially that

13

most common variety, the drunken tongue), she had not coughed at all throughout the ordeal, and there was not a trace of fever.

"You're nervous about yourself, my good woman," I said, "which in your case surprises me; you're too hard a worker to have such fancies."

"Still, them are the symptoms," she answered, doggedly, "and I want a prescription." And she held out her hand, with eighteenpence in it. Such is not the fee in Wimpole Street, but in the East End we are less exacting; and we have the same excuse for taking less as the barrister gave for taking half a crown instead of a guinea; it is often all our clients have in the world.

"I don't want your money, Rebecca, any more than you want my prescription," I said.

"For mercy's sake give it me," she cried, imploringly. "It's not for me, sir; it's for my sister."

"For your sister? I did not know you had a sister. How is it possible for me to prescribe for a patient I have never seen?"

"She is ill, sir, deadly ill," she pleaded.

"The more reason I should see her."

"But she will not see *you*, sir; she made me promise that I would not bring you. She has seen no one but me for years. She's an invalid."

"Well, of course, and has an invalid's fancies, no doubt. Come, take me to her." And I took up my hat.

Then, to my amazement, the big, strong woman burst into tears. "Oh, sir, you don't understand me," she sobbed. "She is not accustomed to be seen like this; you will break her heart."

"Pooh, pooh!" I said; "on the contrary, it is my business to mend it."

Not that I had the least belief in what she said; for, indeed, I began to think that her

sister might be a *lusus naturæ*, of which I had
seen more than one in my East End practice.
Poor creatures that were not good enough, or
bad enough, for a show; two-headed nightin-
gales who had just missed their chance, as it
were, by half a head; elephant-men with imperfectly developed trunks.   When poverty
goes hand-in-hand with disfigurement, it cannot close door and window, or hide in secluded
grounds; but, still, it will shrink from observation all it can, like some shy creature on the
seashore whose shell is too small for it.

Seeing it was useless to argue with me,
Rebecca led the way to Star Court.   Dry,
dusty, airless, but without sunshine—because
the tall black houses are huddled too close
together—it was, indeed, a cheerless spot for
the sound, far more for the sick to dwell in.
A few ragged children were dancing in the
centre of it round a barrel-organ, to the super-
ficial eye an example of how happiness is found

in every spot. But well I knew that in more
than one of these abodes lay women and
children down with fever, to each of whom
every note of the instrument was torture. But
there was no liveried footman there to warn
the unwelcome musician, or policeman to bid
him "move on"—the police in that neighbourhood had their hands full of more serious
matters. Up three flights of stairs we went,
steep enough to suggest the aid of the banisters had they been less grimy and slimy,
and at last into an attic with a sloping roof.

At the first glance, I thought a sunbeam had
found its way there; but it was only a head
of golden hair upon a coarse pillow. The face
was turned to the wall, and Rebecca held her
finger up—stained with toil and rough with
work—to warn me that the invalid was sleeping.

Why I noted the finger was because of the
contrast it exhibited to the thin, white, delicate
hand that lay outside the blanket, for counter-

pane there was none. There was a marriage-
ring on the hand, and it was the only article
in the room which would have fetched a shilling at the pawnbroker's. There was a chair,
but it had no back, and a deal table, one leg
of which, much shorter than the others, was
supplemented by a brick. Upon it stood a
mug with wallflowers in it, the only decoration
the apartment could boast. Yet all was scru-
pulously clean down to the bare boards, unre-
lieved by a shred of carpet. I had seen
hundreds of homes before shorn of every comfort, but never one so cared for in its last
extremity by hand and eye. Even the brick
on which the table stood was washed, and
resembled one from a child's toy-box.

"That is a good sign, her sleeping, is it not,
sir?" whispered Rebecca, eagerly. We had
entered very softly, and doubtless the ear of
the invalid had only caught the footstep she
expected; but when her sister spoke, she
answered, in faint, reproachful tones—

"I am not asleep; and you have broken your word, Rebecca."

"It was not my fault, my darling, indeed it wasn't. Oh! did I not tell you, doctor, how it would be?" And the great gaunt woman wrung her hands distressfully.

"It was not your sister's fault that I am here," I interposed gently. "She would have had me believe she had come to consult me on her own account, but I saw through her. It was my duty to come, and it will be a pleasure to me if I can do you any good."

I had caught sight for a moment of the face of an angel, or rather, as it seemed to me, of one who was about to join the heavenly choir; but even while I was speaking she had put up both her hands before it. It was a poor protection, for they were so thin and fragile that one could almost see through them, but the gesture was eloquent enough.

"You need not be afraid of the doctor, my

dear; he is not like any one else," said Rebecca, soothingly. A compliment evidently addressed to my profession, and not to myself. " She'll come round after a bit, sir," she whispered encouragingly ; " but she has not seen a stranger—not to speak to—for years, and your coming is a terrible trial to her."

I nodded indifferently, as though such shyness was a common trait; for it is a point of honour with us doctors never to be surprised, but to say, "just so," and incline the head at the angle of assent, when a case is introduced to us, whether it be mumps or the leprosy. Moreover, I could have waited patiently for some time to get a glimpse of that face again. It was the face of a girl rather than of a young woman, though, paradoxical as this may seem, there was little of youth in it. The continuance of some distressing emotion, or possibly of physical pain, had, as it will do, driven youth away from it, and instead of " the ver-

meil hue of health," had given it an unnatural
flush, as if autumn had laid its fiery finger on
a ' leaf of springtime; but the features were
perfect, and the large blue eyes the most
beautiful I had ever beheld. They had only
expressed shrinking and affright at my presence, but it was easier to imagine them as the
natural homes of love and tenderness. Around
this picture, the beauty of which had something
unearthly about it, or rather, as it struck my
professional eye, was only to be for a short
time on earth, that gleaming hair made a
golden frame.

A greater contrast to her sister it was not
possible for one woman to be to another.
Presently she seemed to recover herself a little,
and I ventured to put to her a few questions
founded upon what Rebecca had told me. She
answered them very gently, but in so different
a tone that they might well, as in her case,
have had no personal application. This was

a bad sign ; for her disease was consumption, where, if the patient is not, as usual, sanguine, or has little interest in the result, the outlook is gloomy indeed. After recommending several things, which I simply said should be sent in, I took my leave. Rebecca followed me out of the room.

" She does not understand," she whispered piteously. " You must not think her ungrateful, sir. Her mind—— " she hesitated.

" Is fixed on other things than food and physic," I said, smiling. " It is a common case with one so ill as she is."

" She is not dying, doctor ? "

The woman's swarthy face grew pale, and her eyes distended with sheer terror. I had seen relatives anxious about the fate of their dear ones, upon grounds the most momentous —spiritual considerations—but never one so moved as this one ; and yet she did not strike me as being a religious woman. As a rule the

very poor take these matters with philosophy,
as well they may. If there is another world
(which they do not always believe) to which
their invalid is going, it naturally strikes them
that it needs must be an improvement on the
one he is leaving ; and at all events there will
be one less to feed and clôthe. But in the case
of Rebecca, her emotion was infinitely deeper
than mere anxiety or regret; it seemed to
shake the very roots of her being.

"I do not say your sister is dying, my good
woman," I replied. " My examination of her, as
you know, has been very slight; but I confess
that her condition impresses me unfavourably.
She seems to be in very low spirits about
herself."

" Heaven help her, well she may be," groaned
Rebecca.

" And yet she does not seem alarmed as
some do."

" Alarmed ? What has she to be afraid of?

It is others, like me, who have to be afraid. She has done no wrong; if there is a heaven above, she must needs go there."

"Well, that, after all, is the great thing, and should give you comfort, for you will meet again."

I was a young man at the time, with such platitudes at the tip of my tongue. That they are all well meant is the best that can be said of them. When a child is going to school for the first time, we say "the months will soon pass;" when a friend is emigrating for his health, "in a few years we shall see you again strong and well," and since, under these circumstances, this "vacant chaff well-meant for grain" is found to be inefficacious, how can it be otherwise when the separation is complete, the bourne whither our dear one is bound one from which there is no return, and our rejoining him without date, and doubtful? A clergyman may say these things; from his

mouth they may have their effect ; but though
" Never " is a hard word, we have most of us
to bear it. From the doctor, at all events, a
glance of the eye, and a touch of the hand in
token of human sympathy, are, it is my experience, more welcome to the mother that is
about to be childless, to the wife that is about
to be a widow, than this vague consolation.

" ' Comfort,' and ' meet again,' " she echoed,
with a sort of contemptuous despair, and
shaking her head, like one with the palsy,
re-entered the sick-room.

The whole situation amazed and perplexed
me. On all other topics the woman was what
one would have expected her to be. Save for a
somewhat exceptional honesty, cleanliness, and
diligence, Rebecca Bent was like other charwomen ; but in all that pertained to her sister,
she was tender and emotional to an extraordinary degree. I made inquiries about them
without eliciting much information. They had

lived in Star Court for nearly three years, but Rebecca alone was known to their fellow-lodgers. Her sister had been always a recluse, if not an invalid; she had never left the room; it was understood that she took in needlework, when she could obtain employment, which was not often; but Rebecca was the bread-winner. She toiled early and late, but no one had heard a word of complaint from her. As a general rule it is not the hardworkers that complain. It is not that they are resigned to their harsh fate, whatever cant may have to say about it; it is not in human nature to be that; but there is often a certain grim reticence about them; a not unjustifiable resentment.

This was not the case with Rebecca, however. She had her reasons (as I afterwards discovered) for liking work for its own sake. Work preserves us from thinking. She was quiet in her ways, and kept herself *to* herself; but she had a temper of her own. A neigh-

bour once condoled with her on having a sick
sister to keep. " She didn't seem to help much ;
couldn't she put her own shoulder to the wheel
a little more ? There didn't seem so very much
the matter with her," and so on. Then
Rebecca broke out, and exhibited quite an
unexpected command of language. She impressed upon that neighbour the desirability of
minding her own business in such convincing
terms that nobody ever ventured to sympathize
with her upon the labour question again. But
she had not been popular before, and this
ebullition set society against her. She was for
the future very severely let alone.

Gaunt and grim though she was, for my
part, strange to say, Rebecca interested me, at
least as much as my patient, notwithstanding
her many advantages. Her beauty was of the
kind that is heightened rather than otherwise
by delicacy of constitution ; even disease only
rendered it more exquisite. It reminded me

of the lily of the vale, " whom youth makes so
fair, and passion so frail, that the light of its
tremulous bells is seen through their pavilions
of tender green," so transparent was its
splendour. That she was dying I had now no
doubt, nor could the end be far distant. The
spectacle was very touching, even to a professional eye ; but what, I confess, lessened my
sympathy for her was her conduct towards
Rebecca. She seemed to take everything she
did for her as a matter of course. It was quite
true that she gave one the impression of belonging to quite another and a higher sphere of
being ; but to see her so self-conscious of it was
deplorable. If she had been a princess she
could hardly have been served, not only with
more devotion, but with more respectful
reverence. I noticed in particular that, though
Rebecca lavished every term of endearment
upon her sister, she never addressed her by her
Christian name, and I only discovered it to be
Lucy by direct inquiry.

With the selfish egotism of the habitual invalid every doctor is familiar; but with Lucy Bent it was carried beyond all bounds. I had supplied her with various little luxuries, and made arrangements by which, during her illness, her sister should not be under the necessity of leaving her; and for this she expressed herself—though, I have reason to believe, only at Rebecca's prompting—in a few sufficiently suitable words; if she had not uttered them I should have thought little of it. There was not much graciousness in Star Court, though, in this case, where the casket was so fair, one naturally looked for the jewel; but the ignoring of her sister's claim to gratitude, and the coldness—as it seemed to me, the studied coldness —of her manner towards her was painful to witness. She never exchanged a word with her that was not absolutely necessary. Her state was such that it was impossible to remonstrate with her upon that or any other

14

subject; indeed—and, so far, this was an excuse for her—she was so wrapt in her own wretchedness, so given over to, I know not what of regretful and despairing memories, that she seemed to pay no attention even to her own condition, to "the body that did her such grievous wrong," or to the soul that was about to quit it.

Rebecca, on her side, was equally silent; dumb as the dog who, treated with indifference by some morose master, still waits on and watches him with patient devotion, but it was easy to see how she longed for a kind word, or even a loving glance; and longed in vain. At last, when the end was very near, I could forbear no longer; it was a clergyman's business, perhaps, more than mine, but my patient had declined—and with no little vehemence for one so weak—to see a clergyman; and I took my courage (for, strange as it may seem, it needed courage) in both hands, and spoke to her.

" Have you not one word, even of farewell, Lucy, for the sister who has nursed you so tenderly ? "

There was a struggle within the panting bosom, added to the fight for breath, but the lips moved, and what they formed was the monosyllable " No ;" in the faint sound I recognized a distant touch of bitterness.

" I know not what you have suffered," I went on, " and it may be " (this struck me for the first time) " even at her hands; but I know what *she* has suffered, and is suffering now for your sake. Forgive her, if she has done you wrong, as you yourself hope to be forgiven. Look at her, it may be for the last time, and bid her kiss you."

Into the dying eyes, as she turned them on her sister, there came a look of ineffable sweetness ; and she feebly stretched her arms towards her in invitation of an embrace.

Rebecca fell on her knees beside the wretched

bed with a cry in which, for the moment, sorrow seemed to have been swallowed up in joy. To have been the witness of what followed would have been a sacrilege, and I left them together.

It may have been their first and last caress, for when I entered the room the next morning it had but one living tenant. The dead girl lay on the bed with her hands crossed "as if praying dumbly over her breast." The words of the poet occurred to me as I looked at her, but it was that line alone which had any application to her case. That she had not fallen, whatever sin she had committed (though she looked an angel), as Hood's unfortunate had done, I felt certain. Her story was no common one of the street and the river. Everything that loving hands could do had been done for her, to the very last service.

Rebecca was wonderfully calm and resigned, and after a few words of sympathy which, perhaps, had better not have been said, for I

could see they tried her firmness, I spoke of
what was necessary. Of course I took upon
myself all the arrangements of the funeral, but
I had to ask her one question about the death-
certificate.

" I do not know your sister's married name,"
I said.

" She was never married," was the unexpected reply.

My eye wandered interrogatively to the wed-
ding-ring upon that delicate finger on which
the needle had left no trace. It had, indeed,
done little work of any kind, but Rebecca only
shook her head.

" Then I will give your sister's maiden name
—Bent."

" She was not my sister, sir; she was no
relative at all. Put Lester."

" No relative ? Then, indeed, Rebecca, you
may say you have done your duty to your
neighbour."

"My duty!" she answered with bitter scorn; and throwing up her great hands. "It was I who murdered her."

It was not till some days afterwards, when Lucy had been laid to rest in the cemetery, that I heard from Rebecca what she believed to be the story of her crime. It was exaggerated, emotional, and, I am very sure, represented the case only as it appeared to a mind full of remorse and self-reproach.

I prefer, for truth's sake as well as hers, to give the facts as they would have struck an unprejudiced observer.

Lucy Lester was the daughter of a tradesman, well to do, and who had made his money honestly enough; but he was a puritan, and of the strictest sect of the Pharisees. His wife had died when Lucy was still a child, and she was brought up in an atmosphere of gloom and dulness, very unsuited to her character, which was at once frivolous and egotistic. Her beauty,

of which she was only too conscious, was pronounced by the formal society with which she
mixed, to be a snare (as indeed it proved to be),
and every amusement to which she was naturally inclined was sternly forbidden to her.
Rebecca, who had been her nurse, and when
she grew up become her maid, sympathized
with her young mistress, to whom she was also
genuinely attached, and made common cause
with her against her persecutors, as she called
them, though those included her parent himself.
He was very thrifty, and kept Lucy "short" as
to pin-money, and Rebecca, who, as she told me
(for she spared herself in nothing), "was very
greedy of gain," on a very low scale of wages.
It was a sad and rather sordid story of severity
and repression met by duplicity and intrigue.
What redeemed it was the disinterested though
exaggerated fealty of Rebecca, which would
have borne comparison with that of feudal
times. Except for her singular beauty there

was nothing admirable in Lucy, who indeed was proud, selfish, and exacting, but in Rebecca's eyes she was perfection, and a martyr; fit for a prince, but with no choice of suitors, save of a commonplace and unworthy kind, who never having seen a stage play had no notion of the desirability of making a friend of the maid of their mistress.

Presently, however, a lover appeared of quite another stamp, but unhappily a clandestine lover. Mr. Power was one of her father's customers, a gentleman, as was understood, of good position, who at all events gave large orders which were punctually paid for, and while calling on Mr. Lester on business he chanced to catch sight of Lucy, and became at once enamoured of her beauty. Without the simplicity which is the safeguard of her sex, she was absolutely ignorant of that world with which she panted to mingle; the man's air of fashion made as much way with her as his protestations; and unfor-

tunately the lavishness which a man of his
stamp displays, when bent on such a design,
was taken by Rebecca as a sign of a generous
nature ; without knowing them (as I think) to
be exactly bribes, she took his bribes.

With one word to her master she could probably have saved his daughter, but she did not
feel she was in danger.   Even a word of warning to Lucy herself might not have been thrown
away, but she did not give it.   On the contrary, urged by many considerations, dislike of
her master and his surroundings, willingness to
please her darling, and confidence in Power's
professions, she assisted him to elope with her.
I am afraid there was even a time when Lucy
shrank from the audacity of that design, and
but for Rebecca would have abandoned it ; but
it was because she was herself deceived.   Indeed, at the last, when Lucy had lost her head
as well as her heart, and would have risked all
for love, Rebecca stepped in, and insisted upon

being present at the marriage ceremony. It was a barren precaution—though poor Lucy might afterwards have used it as a weapon of revenge, if she had had the heart for revenge— for in a few weeks she discovered that he whom she had believed to be her husband was a married man. In that brief space she had lost all; fortune, friends, and home; for her father closed his doors against her; and the unhappy girl found herself thrown on her own resources, which consisted only of a scanty wardrobe and a few jewels. Then, like a wounded tigress, she turned upon Rebecca, with " It is you who have been my ruin."

The fury that might reasonably have been poured on her deceiver seemed quenched in the very catastrophe he had caused, as flame deserts the blackened ruin; so far as he was concerned the crime of which she had been the victim was so overwhelming that in place of indignation she felt only wretchedness and despair; too

weak to seek relief in self-destruction, she yet
desired to hide herself from her fellow-creatures,
and especially to be seen no more of men.

What remained to her of vitality took the
form of passionate reproach of her late ally and
assistant, and not a word did Rebecca say in
her own defence.

Instead of leaving her young mistress to a
fate only too easy to be foreseen, she devoted
herself with penitence and remorse to smooth
the rough road she must needs travel for the
future.

Effort of her own Lucy never made, and
accepted the other's services not only as her
due, but as but a small instalment of the
obligation she had incurred in having given her
such bad advice. That she had not forgiven
her she made very plain, even (as has been
shown) up to the last moment of her life; but
Rebecca never thought herself hardly used.

"There was nothing I could do, as you may

believe," she said, " that deserved thanks. It
was owing to me that my poor dear mistress,
so young, so beautiful, so tender, had fallen
into the hands of a villain, and unfit as she was
to bear hardships, was compelled to live upon a
crust. Was it to my credit that these hands
which had taken his bribes, provided the
crust ? "

If Miss Lucy had complained, she said she
could have better borne the consciousness of her
crime ; but, after that first outbreak, she kept
silence, a cold reproachful silence that for years
had chilled the other's very heart. All she
stipulated for was to be alone, not to be spoken
to, not to be seen, and, even when her illness
had become severe, it was only on Rebecca's
promise to obtain professional advice without
the doctor's presence that the sick girl had
permitted her to apply to me.

This was the story of Rebecca's remorse.

I did what I could to reason with the poor

LUCY LESTER'S GRAVE.

woman, by pointing out how penance atones for wrong ; but if I had not been so fortunate as to obtain for her Lucy's death-bed forgiveness, she would certainly never have forgiven *herself.* As it was, she was in some degree comforted. I got her a situation in the country with some friends of mine, where she was greatly esteemed, and remained for years. She always took a day or two's holiday in the summer. No one knew where she spent it, for she had no friends ; but at the same time, who ever visited a certain East End cemetery would have found, on Lucy Lester's grave, fresh flowers.

IS IT A MAN?

By J. M. BARRIE.

I.

J. M. BARRIE.

I CAME upon his grave accidentally a few weeks ago while taking a short cut through the cemetery of an unlovely provincial town. His name I had forgotten the night I heard it years ago; I heard it years ago; had flung it away, so to speak, with the handbills he gave me at the same time, but the wording on the tombstone recalled his story to me as vividly as if it was a long lost friend

whom I had suddenly struck against. I laughed
at the story when he told it to me, but when
I read it in brief on the tombstone I wondered
why I had laughed.

We only met once, and it was in London
at the theatre. His stall adjoined mine.
When his lips were at rest he was a melancholy
looking little man, but frequently he spoke to
himself, and then all character went out of his
face. For a time he paid no attention to the
acting, but by-and-by he sat up excitedly in
his seat, rubbed his hands nervously on his
trousers, and leaning in my direction, peered,
not at the stage, but at the wings. I heard
him mutter, " Her cue in a moment, and I
don't see her ! " He looked around the house
as if to signal to everybody that something was
about to happen, and then I noticed his feet
begin to beat the floor instinctively, and his
one palm run to the other. Next moment the
heavy father whispered to the old, and there-

fore comic spinster, " But not a word of this
to my daughter; here she comes."

The heroine of the piece sailed on to the
stage, with tears for her father and smiles for
the audience, and, as I thought, one quick
glance for my neighbour. His feet pattered
softly on the floor, as a sign to the audience
to cheer, but they were reluctant, and after she
had given them an imploring glance, she
began to speak slowly, as one saying to herself
between her spoken words, " I am still quite
willing to stop if you will applaud me." And
she was applauded, for my neighbour's feet at
last set others a-going, and then she curtseyed
and waited for more, and then we all became
energetic. The little man had been breathing
quick in his excitement, but now he heaved
a great sigh of relief, and whispered to me
in exultation, " What a reception the O'Reilly
has got, sir, and quite spontaneous. The
same thing occurs every night, every night,

every night! Hush! you will see acting
now."

He had silenced me when I was about to ask
him if he was here every night. I judged him
an ardent admirer of Miss O'Reilly, and had
further evidence during the first act that one
man may lead the applause as a conductor
leads the orchestra. When Miss Helmsley
entered, and some pittites began to cheer, my
neighbour cried "Sh-sh" so fiercely that the
demonstration stopped abruptly, and Miss
Helmsley withdrew her curtsey. When the
heavy father stopped in the middle of his
long speech for a "hand" to help him on his
way, he would have got it but for the "Sh-sh"
of the little man. When the comedian nudged
the elderly spinster in the ribs, which is how
elderly spinsters are made love to on the stage,
some ladies giggled, but my neighbour looked
at them with a face that said, "There is nothing
funny in that," and they restrained their mirth.

But when Miss O'Reilly snatched the smoking-cap from Leonard and put it on her own flaxen head, he chuckled till the whole audience admitted the fun of it, and when Miss O'Reilly told Lord John to stand back and let her pass, my neighbour brought down the house; and when she made her reluctant exit he brought down the house again ; and when the curtain fell on the first act he shouted "O'Reilly" until we were all infected. Not until he had her before the curtain would he retire, and then it was to speak about her to me. The exchange of a vesta introduced us to each other.

"You have seen the piece before?" I asked, with the good-nature that is born of a cigarette. I had already sufficient interest in him to wonder who he was.

"The piece?" he echoed indifferently. "Oh yes; I have seen the greater part of it frequently."

"How does it end?"

He shrugged his shoulders.

" I don't know," he answered contemptuously. "I always walk out of the house just before the last tableau."

" Is Miss O'Reilly not on the stage in that tableau ? " I asked.

" She is not," he replied, rapping out an oath or two, and trembling with rage. " Did you ever hear of anything so monstrous ? She is leading lady, the idol of the town, and yet she is not on at the end. Excuse me, sir. I am always taken in this way when I think of it."

He bit his cigarette in two and asked for another vesta. Then he explained.

" She dies, you know, in the middle of the act."

" Ah, that accounts for it," I said.

" Not at all," he retorted ; " she ought not to die until the tableau. And if she had to die then, that should have been the tableau. What do people come to the theatre to see ? "

" The play," I suggested.

" Pooh, the play ! " he sneered. " There are twenty plays to be seen nightly at West End theatres, but only one O'Reilly. They come to see the O'Reilly, sir, and it is defrauding the public to let her die a moment before the end."

" Still," I said, " the author—— "

" Pshaw ! " he broke in, " who thinks of the author ? He could easily have brought down the curtain on the O'Reilly's death, and I am confident he meant to do it. But Helmsley is the management's niece, and insisted on being the only lady in the tableau. You noticed that Helmsley was a complete frost ? I distinctly heard some one hissing her."

" So did I," I said, smiling, for the some one had been himself.

" You heard it too," he cried audaciously. " Thank you, sir," he said, and shook me warmly by the hand.

" The O'Reilly herself," he added, " had no

wish to be in the tableau, but she knew the public would expect it. She is a woman, that, sir."

" She is," I agreed.

" Ha ! " he exclaimed. " You, too, were struck by it ? But she impresses every one in the same way. The management pay her a princely salary ; but she is worth it. Did you hear how that man in the pit laughed over her lines about bread and cheese and kisses? I wonder who he is ? "

" What salary does she get ? " I asked, with the curiosity of a theatre-goer.

" They say," he replied, looking at me sharply, " that she gets eighty pounds a week."

" Hem ! " I said.

He coughed. " What a carriage she has ! " he exclaimed ; and then waited for me to agree.

" Wonderful ! " I said, for I never contradict a man who is in love.

" You think she has a wonderful carriage ? "

he asked, as if I had put the idea into his head.
" Yes, you are quite right. I will tell her
you remarked on it."

" You know her personally ? "

"I have that honour," he replied with
dignity. " Candidly now, is not her education
superb ? "

" It is," I said.

" I agree with you," he answered, "and you
have used the one word that properly describes
it. Superb! Yes, that is the very word. I
will tell her you said superb. I see you know
acting, sir, when you see it. Not that I would
call it acting. Would you call it acting ? "

" Certainly not," I answered recklessly, but
hoping he would not ask me to give it a name.

" No," he said, " it is not acting. It is
simply genius."

" Genius," I said from memory, " is all the
talents in a nutshell."

" Ha ! " he cried, " that is how you would

describe her? All the talents in a nutshell!
What a capital line for the advertisements.
All the talents in a nutshell! I will tell her
you said that about her."

He lowered his voice. "Press?" he asked
with some awe. I shook my head.

"Got friends on the press?" he next
inquired.

"Yes," I said, remembering that a pressman
owed me five pounds.

"Critics?"

"I shouldn't wonder."

"Then," he said eagerly, "put them up to
that line, 'all the talents in a nutshell.' Or
stop; would you mind giving me their private
address?"

"Unfortunately, I cannot."

"That is a pity, because if you could see
your way to a 'par,' I think I might be able
to introduce you to the O'Reilly. But she is
very particular."

"You are an enthusiast about her," I remarked.

"Who could help it?" he answered. "I have watched her career since she was—on my soul, sir, since she was nobody in particular. There was a time when that woman was no more famous than you are. You were speaking of her genius a minute ago, but, would you believe it, she rose from the ranks, positively from the ranks."

If I had swooned at this, his hands would have been ready to catch me ; but I kept my senses.

"Your interest in her," I ventured to say, "was very natural, but it must have taken up a good deal of your time."

"All my time," he said.

"Except during business hours, of course."

"From the time I rise until midnight."

"Then you have no profession?"

"That is my profession."

"I USED TO BE IN THE PROFESSION MYSELF," HE SAID, SIGHING. "I AM JOLLY LITTLE JIM!"

" What ? "

" The interest I take in her."

" And did you never do anything else ? " I asked, beginning to envy the little man his father.

At once the melancholy look, of which I have spoken, came back to his face.

"I used to be in the profession myself," he said, sighing. "I am Jolly Little Jim."

He did not look it at that moment.

"You have forgotten me, I see," he said, dolefully. "Think a moment. Jolly Little Jim was the name."

"I am afraid I never heard it," I had to admit.

" Nonsense ! " he answered testily. " Everybody knew that name once. I got no other, though my real name is James Thorpe. Why, I advertised as Jolly Little Jim. You *must* have heard it."

" Perhaps I have," I replied, pitying his distress.

"If you would care to read my press notices," he began putting his hand into his pocket, "I can—— "

"Not to-night," I interposed hurriedly.

"I can repeat most of them," he said brightly.

"Rather tell me why you gave up a profession," I said, "which you doubtless adorned."

"Thank you," he answered, again pressing my hand. "Well, sir, the O'Reilly has the responsibility for that."

"You gave up acting because it interfered with your interest in her?"

"You may put it in that way. I gave up everything for her. If that woman, sir, had asked me to choose between her and my press notices, I believe I would have burned them."

"How has she rewarded you?" I asked, seeing that he was of a communicative nature.

"She married me," he answered, drawing himself up to his full height. "Yes, I am her husband!"

It was I who shook his hand this time. I
could think of nothing else to do. He was
beginning his story, when the bell tinkled,
warning us to return to our seats.

"She is on immediately," he said, "so we
must go back and give her a hand. I'll meet
you here again after the second act."

II.

DURING the second act Mr. Thorpe behaved as
previously, drinking in Miss O'Reilly's every
word, cheering her comings and goings, and
yawning, and even reading a newspaper, when
he should have been listening to Miss Helmsley.
Once I saw him make a note on his programme,
and felt sure it was, "All the talents in a nutshell." I started him on his story as soon as
he joined me in the smoking-room. (He had
remained in his seat to shout "O'Reilly.")

"The first time I ever set eyes on her," he

began, "was at Dublin, where we had both been engaged for pantomime. Yes, that woman once played in pantomime; and, what is more, she was only second girl. That is a strange thing to think of. I was the first villain, Deepdyeo, and the *Shamrock* said of my creation, ' Another part admirably rendered is the Deepdyeo of Mr. James Thorpe, better known to fame as Jolly Little Jim. Mr. Thorpe, who was received with an ovation——' "

" But you were to tell me of Miss O'Reilly," I reminded him.

" Ah," he said, " I shall never forget that first meeting. It took place at rehearsal, and when I left the theatre that afternoon I was a changed man."

" You fell in love with her at first sight ? "

" Not absolutely at first sight. You see, I was introduced to her before the rehearsal began, and there was no opportunity of falling in love with her then."

" Still, she had impressed you ? "

" How could she impress me before I had seen her do anything ? What is it in a woman that one falls in love with ? "

" Who can tell ? " I said.

" Anybody can tell," he answered, putting me down for a bachelor. " It is the genius in her, or rather what we consider genius, for many men make a mistake about that."

" So you loved her for her genius ? "

" What first struck me was her exit. I suppose I may say that I fell in love with it at once. Then she sang; only a verse, but it was enough. Later she danced, and that, sir, was a revelation. I knew the woman was a genius. By the time the pantomime was in full swing, she was the one woman in the world for me."

" And she had fallen in love with your genius, too ? "

" I could not be certain. You see, we

were not on speaking terms; she was so jealous."

"But that," I said, "is recognized as a sign of love. No doubt, she wanted you entirely to herself. Who was the lady?"

"What lady?" he asked, in surprise.

"The lady Miss O'Reilly was jealous of," I said.

"I never said she was jealous of a lady; though, of course, she would be jealous of the principal girl. I spoke of myself."

"But how," I questioned, "could she be jealous unless she thought you were paying attention to some other woman?"

"Oh!" he said, with slow enlightenment, "I see what you mean, but you don't see what I mean. It was of me that she was jealous, or rather of my song. You may not be aware that in pantomime we are allowed to choose our own songs. Well, it so happened that she and I both wanted to sing the same song. It was an exquisite thing, called, 'Do you think when you wink?' and as I had applied for permission to sing it first she was told to select something else. That was why we did not speak."

"But if you loved her," I said, speaking, it is true, on a subject of which I knew little, "you would surely have consented to waive your rights to the song. Love, it is said, delights in self-sacrifice."

"No doubt," he admitted, "but you know the lines, 'I could not love you, dear, so much, loved I not honour more.' Well, my honour was at stake, for I had promised my admirers in Dublin — and they were legion (see the *Shamrock* for January 12, 1883)—to sing that song. And my fame was at stake as well as my honour, for I created quite a furore with 'Do you think when you wink?'"

"Still," I insisted, "love is all powerful."

"I admit it," he answered, "and, what is

more, I proved it, for after I had sung the song a week, I transferred it to her."

" Did she sing it as well as you had done ? "

There was a mighty struggle within him before he could reply, but when he did speak he was magnificent.

" She sang it far better than I," he said firmly, and then winced.

" It was a great sacrifice you made," I said gently, " but doubtless it had its reward. Did she give you her hand in exchange for the song ? "

" No," he answered, " we were not married until a year after that. She was grateful to me, but soon we quarrelled again. The fact is that I took a 'call' which she insisted was meant for her. She felt that disappointment terribly; indeed, she has not got over it yet. She cannot speak about it without crying."

" You mean," I said, " that you years ago deprived her of the privilege of curtseying to an audience ? Surely she would not let that prey on her mind ? "

" You don't understand," he replied, " that fame is food and drink to an artist. It was months before she forgave me that, though she is naturally the most tender-hearted creature. Our baggage man stole fifty pounds from her, and she would not prosecute him because she knew his sister. But you see it was not money that I deprived her of—it was fame."

" And did you win your way back into her favour ? " I asked, " by letting her take a ' call ' that was meant for you ? "

" No," he said; " several times I determined to do so, but when the moment came I could not make the sacrifice. I spent about half my salary in presents to her; but, although she took them, she refused to listen to any proposal of marriage. By this time I had confessed my love for her. Well, we parted, and soon afterwards I got an engagement as chief

16

comedian in the 'Powder Monkey' Company, which was then on tour. She was playing chambermaid in it. Fancy that woman flinging herself away on chambermaids! I made a big hit in my part. The *Lincoln Observer* said, 'Mr. James Thorpe, the celebrated Jolly Little Jim, created a——' "

"But about Miss O'Reilly," I asked.

"We got on swimmingly at first," he said.

"She had decided to forgive you?"

"No, she was stiff the first day, but I put her up to a bit of business, that used to be encored nightly, and then she accepted my offer of marriage. But a week after I had given her the engagement-ring she returned it to me. I don't blame her."

"You admit that she had just cause of complaint against you?"

"Yes; no woman who was an artist could have stood it. The fact is, that one night I took the 'up' side of her in our comic love scene. That is to say, I had my face to the audience, and so she was forced to turn her back to them. I had no right to do it, but a sort of madness came over me, and I yielded to the impulse. As soon as we had made our exits she flung the ring in my—ah, she gave me back the ring, and, for the remainder of the tour, she was not civil to me. The tour ended abruptly ; indeed, the manager decamped, owing us all a fortnight's salary, and we were stranded in Bootle without money to pay for our lodgings, not to speak of our tickets back to London. I pawned my watch and sold my fur coat, and shared what I got for them with her."

" And so the engagement was resumed ? "

"No, no ; that was merely a friendly act, and it was accepted as such. The engagement was not resumed until I got a 'par' about her into a Sunday paper. But that is the bell again. I'll tell you the rest after her death scene."

Miss O'Reilly died as slowly as the management would allow her, and, when she had gasped her last gasp with her hair down, Jolly Little Jim that was led the tears and the cheers, cried out, "Superb, by Jove! that woman has all the talents in a nut-shell," and strutted from the stalls in a manner that invited the rest of the audience to follow. But everybody, save Mr. Thorpe and myself, remained to see the comic man produce the missing will, and so my little friend and I got the smoking-room to ourselves.

"The next time we were on tour together," he continued, after I had given the death scene a testimonial, "was in 'Letters of Fire,' with a real steam-engine. I was Bill Rody, the returned convict, and the *Rochester Age* said, 'Mr. Thorpe, who, as Jolly Little Jim, made such a——'"

"The engagement was resumed by this time?" I asked.

"I told you the 'par' had done that. However, we had another tiff during rehearsals, because I got the epilogue to speak. I dare say that would have led to a rupture had not——"

"Had not she loved you so deeply," I suggested.

"She loved me fondly," he replied, "but she loved fame more. Every true genius does. No, the reason she did not break with me then was that I was 'on' in her great scene in the fourth act. You see, as chief comedian I had a right to a little comic by-play in that scene, and if I had exercised that right I should have drawn away attention from herself. Thus I had the whip hand of her. I am inclined to think that had I pressed the point I could have married her during the run of that piece."

"By threatening, if she delayed the wedding,

to introduce comic business into her great scene?"

"Yes; but I did not, and you are no doubt wondering why. The fact is, I thought my self-denial would soften her heart and so bring about the results I was pining for. Perhaps it would have done so, but unfortunately, 'Letters of Fire' did not draw (though a great success artistically), and we had to put 'London Slums' on in its place. In that piece the leading juvenile played up to her so well that she began to neglect me. I was in despair, and so not quite accountable for my actions. Nevertheless, you will think the revenge I took as cold-blooded as it seemed to her. You must understand that, though our pieces were splendidly billed, the O'Reilly had fifty chromos of herself, done at her own expense, and all framed. These she got our agent in advance to exhibit in the best places in the best shops, and undoubtedly they added to her fame. They preceded us by a week, and so she was always well known before we opened anywhere. Well, sir, 1 got fifty chromos of myself framed, and ten days before we were due at Sheffield I had them put into fifty barbers' shops there."

" Why barbers' shops ? " I interposed.

" Because they are most seen and discussed there," he explained. " It comes natural to a man when he is being shaved to talk about what is on at the theatres. I can't say why that is so, but so it is. Perhaps one reason is that barbers are nearly always enthusiasts on matters of art. Well, if there is a good chromo in the shop, of course it comes in for its share of discussion, and the barber tells what parts you have played before, and so on. It is a great help. However, the O'Reilly no sooner heard what I had done than she told me all was over between us."

" Still," I said, " the barbers would have had room for her pictures as well as for yours."

"I got the best places," he answered; "and there is this, too, to consider. The more chromos there are to look at, the less attention does any particular one get; and she held that if I loved her truly I would not have stepped in, as it were, between her and the public. She did not get a reception that opening night at Sheffield, and, of course, she gave me the blame. It seriously affected her health."

"But you made that quarrel up?"

"Not for three weeks. Then she gave in. Instead of my going to her, she came to me and offered to renew the engagement if I would withdraw my chromos."

"Which you did gladly, of course?"

"I took a night to think of it. You who are not an artist cannot conceive how I loved my chromos. Did I tell you that I had printed beneath them, 'Yours very sincerely, Jolly Little Jim'? However, I did yield to her wishes, and we were to be married at Newcastle,

when a terrible thing happened. We have now
come to the turning-point of my life. At Newcastle, sir, I made my last appearance on the
stage."

Mr. Thorpe turned his face from me until he
recovered command of it. Then he resumed.

" Two days before the marriage was to take
place a Newcastle paper slated her and praised
me. It. said, ' Miss O'Reilly ought to take a
page out of Mr. Thorpe's book. She should
learn from him that the action should suit the
word, not precede it. She should note his
facial expression, which is comedy in picture,
and control her own tendency to let her face
look after itself. She should take note of his
clear pronunciation and model her somewhat
snappy delivery on it.' Sir, I read that notice
with mixed feelings. As an artist I could not
but delight in its complimentary references to
myself, but as a lover I dreaded its effect on the
O'Reilly. After breakfast I went to call on

her at her lodgings, and happening to pass a
number of news-shops on the way, I could not
resist the temptation to buy at each a paper
with the notice. I concealed the papers about
my person, and as I approached her door I
tried to look downcast. But I fear my step
was springy. Perhaps she saw me from her
window. At all events, her landlady informed
me that Miss O'Reilly declined to see me.
' Here is something I was told to give you,'
said the woman, handing me a pill-box. It
contained the ring! I compelled the O'Reilly
to listen to me that night at the theatre, and
she allowed that I was not to blame for the
notice. But she pointed out that there could
be no chance of happiness for a husband and
wife whose interests were opposed, and I saw
that it was true. I walked about the streets of
Newcastle all that night, such was my misery,
such the struggle in my breast between love
and fame. Well, sir, love conquered, as it

never could have conquered her, for she was a great artist, and I only a small one, though the *Basingstoke Magpie* said of me, 'The irresistibly droll Mr. Thorpe, better known as——'"

"The play will end in a minute," I said. "How did you win her?"

"I offered," he replied, with emotion, "to give up my profession and devote myself to furthering her fame."

"And to live on her?" I said aghast.

"You who do not understand art may put it in that way," he replied; "but she realized the sacrifice I was making for her sake, and doubted my love no longer. Was it nothing, sir, to give up my fame, to give up the name I was known by all over England (as the *Torquay Chat* said), and sink to the level of those who have never been mentioned in the papers? Why, you yourself had forgotten the famous Jolly Little Jim."

His voice was inexpressibly mournful, and

I felt that I really had been listening to a love romance. The last three hours, too, had shown me that Mr. Thorpe was responsible for some of the fame of his wife.

" The management," he went on bravely, " allowed me to retire without the usual fort-night's notice, and so the marriage took place on the day we had previously arranged it for."

" Had you a pleasant honeymoon ? " I asked.

" In one sense," he replied, " we had no honeymoon, for she played that night as usual; but in another sense it has been a honeymoon ever since, for we have the same interests, the same joys, the same sorrows."

"That is to say, you have both only her fame to think of now? May I ask, did she, for whom you made such a sacrifice, make any sacrifice for you ? "

" She did indeed," he answered. " For four

weeks she let her name be printed in the bills thus : ' Miss O'Reilly (Mrs. James Thorpe),' though to have it known by the public that she is married is against an actress."

" And you are happy in your new occupation ? "

"Very happy," he answered cheerfully, " and very proud." Then with a heavy sigh he added, " But I wish people would remember Jolly Little Jim."

There was really something pathetic about the man ; but before I could tell a lie and say that I now remembered Jolly Little Jim perfectly, the audience began to applaud, and Mr. Thorpe, thrusting some bills into my hands, hurried back to the stalls to shout " O'Reilly."

As I have said, I never met him again, nor thought of him, until I found myself at his grave. This is the inscription on the tombstone :

ERECTED TO THE MEMORY OF
JAMES THORPE,
AGED 38,

BY HIS SORROWING WIFE,
THE FAMOUS MAY O'REILLY
(Of the principal theatres).

Poor Mr. Thorpe! There was something lovable about him. The O'Reilly might have put on the tombstone: "Better known as Jolly Little Jim." It would have gratified him.

THE GOLDEN RULE.

By Mrs. OLIPHANT.

I.

The breakfast-room in the vicarage at Leighton-Furness was one of the most cheerful rooms you can imagine, especially at the hour and the meal to which it was devoted. It got all the morning sun, and on a warm morning in May, when the lilacs with which the lawn was surrounded were in full bloom, and the pretty breakfast-table was adorned — as all tables are nowadays—with the flowers of the season, wallflowers golden and brown, with the dew still on them freshly gathered, making a glow of colour among the white china, and filling the room with fragrance, you could not have seen a pleasanter place. And the family gathered round the table was in every way suited to the place. First, the vicar, sixty, hale and hearty, with white hair, which was exceedingly becoming to him, and a fine country colour speaking of fresh air and much exercise. Second, his wife, Mrs. Wynyard, ten years younger, very well preserved, who had been a handsome woman in her day; and third, Emily, not, perhaps, to be described in these words, but yet a young woman whose looks were not to be despised, and who would have been an important member of any household in which she had found herself. It was a special providence, Mrs. Wynyard believed, all things considered, that up to this moment her father's house had pleased her more than any other, and that no suitor had carried her away.

For it need scarcely be said that in this pleasant house everything was not pleasant. Had all been well with them the historian would have had nothing to tell ; from whence, no doubt, comes the saying, whether appropriated to countries or to wives, that those are the happiest of whom there is nothing to be said. The post had come in just before the moment at which this episode in their lives opens, and the ladies, as was natural, had thrown themselves upon their letters. The vicar, for his part, had opened his newspaper, which is the natural division—I do not say of labour—in the circumstances. For at sixty a man, and especially a clergyman, gets a little indifferent about his correspondence, which is generally more a trouble than a pleasure ; whereas a woman's interest in her letters, even when they are about nothing in particular, never fails.

This morning, however, there was some special interest which made even the vicar's absorption in his newspaper a little fictitious. When Mrs. Wynyard and her daughter took

17

up the letters, they both in one breath exclaimed "Jack!" throwing aside the other items of their correspondence as if they mattered less than nothing. When he heard that exclamation the vicar looked up from his paper and said, "Well?" sharply, looking from one to another; but receiving no reply after a moment's interval returned, or seemed to return, to his reading. He knew by long experience that Jack's letters generally meant some scrape or other, and he was relieved when he got no answer; but still, I think, his newspaper for the moment was more or less a pretence.

Jack was not a son appropriate to a vicarage: he was not of the kind of those who are their father's favourite and their mother's joy. How it is that this comes to pass, who can tell? With everything to lead him to do well, every tradition and habit of life in his favour, he had not done well. He should have been ready to

step into the vicarage in his father's place, for
it was a sort of family living, securing many
good things to the fortunate inheritor. But
it was soon found that this was out of the
question ; not in the way which is most respect-
able and even superior nowadays, entitling a
young man to the interest and admiration of
everybody — that of religious doubts and
scruples—but in a more vulgar way, which
secures nobody's interest. He had not managed
even to take his degree ; he had done nothing
that he ought to have done : and, instead of
being in orders or at the bar, or a fellow of his
college, all which would have been things
reasonable and to be expected, he was in a
merchant's office in London, sadly against his
will, and against all the prepossessions of his
family. But what was he, then, to do ? Jack
had nothing to suggest : what he would have
liked would have been to do nothing at all, but,
failing that, he did not mind what it was. It

was considered a great piece of luck when his father's old friend, Mr. Bullock, took him into his office at an age when young men are not generally taken into offices, and for a time it was supposed that Jack was going to do very well. But in an evil hour Mr. Bullock sent him on a commercial mission to America, in which Jack was not successful—perhaps because he thought a voyage like that was chiefly a frolic; perhaps for other causes. He had not been successful, but yet, when he returned home (considerably after the time at which he ought to have returned home) he was not dismissed because of his employer's affection for his father. Mr. Bullock, however, took an opportunity of telling the vicar privately that Jack would not do anything in business.

"He may make his own living as a poor clerk," the merchant said, "which is a dreary thing to look forward to. I gave him a chance, but he hasn't taken it. I felt it my duty to tell you, Wynyard : if you can find anything else for him where he may do better, don't hesitate to take him away."

The vicar knew very well this meant that his commercial friend would be glad to get rid of Jack, but he did not take the hint.

"It is always something that he should be making his living," he said, and Mr. Bullock was too great a friend of the Wynyards to send their boy away.

But Jack got on worse than ever after that unsuccessful attempt. As for making his living, his mother knew how many little things there were to be made up. It was a knowledge which the ladies of the family kept as far as they could from his father. But when he got into any bad scrape this was not possible, so that all the members of the family were a little afraid, as well as eager, to see what was in Jack's letters when they came. They did not come very often, and two in one day was a thing which probably had never happened before : the scrape must be graver than usual to warrant such an effort on his part, they all thought. Each of the recipients gave a little gasp on opening her special communication, but neither said anything, which at first was an ease to the vicar's mind. But the letters were long (another wonder), and after a while he became impatient. When Emily had reached the fourth page of hers, which her father saw, in some miraculous way, through the *Times,* he put down his paper altogether and again said, " Well ? " in a still sharper tone.

" Oh, papa ! the most wonderful news," Emily said.

" Well ? " cried Mrs. Wynyard, not to be behind, " I can't tell you if it is well or not, but it is something, at least, that I never thought I should live to see."

" It may be the making of him, mother," cried Emily.

"OH, PAPA! THE MOST WONDERFUL NEWS," EMILY SAID.

" Or his ruin," Mrs. Wynyard said.

" What is it," cried the vicar, bringing down his fist on the table, " in the name of —— ? "

It was only to be expected from a vicar that he should never use any bad words : and neither did he make a free use of those that are too good for common use, and which sound profane, even when authorized, as some people think, by his cloth. But he had a habit of going very near the edge, as if he were about to say them, which had often an impressive effect.

" Papa—I don't know how to tell you—Jack has got engaged."

" Oh, stop, Charles, stop ! wait till you hear. Don't say anything rash. To a lady whom he met in America (I knew there was some reason for his staying so long in America)—a lady — who is rolling in money, Charles ! "

The vicar had his mouth opened to make a remark when he was stopped by his wife ; indeed, he had more than half made it before he could stop himself. "The confounded foo—!" Being arrested, he brought himself up with a run and a gasp.

"Wait till you hear it rightly!" cried his wife. "He met her in some out-of-the-way place; don't you remember he did say something about an out-of-the-way place, Emily? and fell in love with her. But poor boy, he was too honourable to speak. How could he, knowing he had nothing? It is that that has made him so unsettled. Didn't I always say there was something, Emily,—something we didn't know?"

"As for that," said the vicar, getting his breath, "there are probably hundreds of things we don't know."

"Oh, Charles, don't be so harsh; when now there is every appearance—— Her father has come over with her, and has called at the office. They've taken a house in the country, and they've asked Jack to stay with them."

" But more, more, far more ! " cried Emily, crimson with excitement, " he has proposed— and has been accepted, papa."

" Are you sure you are not dreaming all this ? " the vicar said. " Look again ; there must be some mistake."

" There is no mistake at all ; read it yourself," said Mrs. Wynyard, thrusting the letter into his hands. " Of course it is for you as much as me. He says a pretty creature, with those wonderful complexions American girls are said to have, and with Heaven only knows how much money ; oh, I don't wonder your father is flurried ; I cannot get my breath myself."

" It may be the making of him, mother ! "

" If it isn't the other thing," Mrs. Wynyard said.

" How could it be the other thing ? when we have always said between ourselves that a wife, a nice wife, who had sense——, if it were ever possible that he could be able to marry, would be the saving of Jack!"

"Ah, yes," said Mrs. Wynyard, "if he could have had an income to marry on—an income of his own ; but if the money is all on the woman's side, and a father to look after her, to tie it up. Oh, it isn't that I am for money, though I see the great, great advantage. But would she take all the trouble with him if it was like that?"

"She would love to take the trouble," said Emily. "Could she be happy if he were not happy—and right?" she added in an undertone.

The vicar glanced over the letter while this conversation was going on. He did not read it line by line, but jumped at the meaning, having had it already explained to him. And for a moment his heart rose lightly in his breast. To have Jack provided for, suddenly made independent, no longer a trouble and

anxiety to everybody belonging to him, but
with a home, an income, a keeper (so to speak)
of his own! The vicar's heart gave a leap of
relief and delight. No more responsibility.
It would be his wife's business to look after
him, and nobody could do that as well as a
wife. And then the money. Even without
the money, if there had been any chance that
Jack could ever have enough to live upon, they
had all been agreed that a wife might be the
making of him. That meant, I fear, that she
(poor soul! the problematical wife) would take
the anxiety off the shoulders of his parents,
that she would put herself between Jack and
harm, and perhaps cure him, and bring him
right—a thing which it is known women have
undertaken to do, and have done *tant bien que
mal*, and made life possible, before now. This
was an aspiration they had all breathed, never
expecting, however, that it would come to pass
—and to see it suddenly realized, and with

money added, that would make it all the more
sure! A beautiful vision rose before the vicar's
mind—of a time when there would be no
anxiety about Jack, no remittances to send
him, no dreadful news of dismissal to be looked
for, or any other anxiety of that kind; no call
upon every available penny to make up for
some misadventure : but peace and happiness,
and some one to watch over him wherever he
went. The money, indeed, was a great thing,
but the guardian, the companion, the some
one to watch over him, that was the thing
of all.

But then the vicar put down the letter,
and those heartstrings, which had so relaxed
and been sensible of the happiest loosening and
ease, tightened all at once again. He put his
elbows on the table, and his face in his hands.
The ladies were silent, thinking that he was
thanking God. But, when he looked up
after that pause, his face was not the face

of a man glorified by thanksgiving. The old
lines were all drawn again round his anxious
eyes.

"Jane," he said, "and you, Emily, listen to
me. We talk every day, don't we, about doing
to our neighbours as we would that our neighbours should do to us?"

"Surely," said Mrs. Wynyard, a little dismayed, though she scarcely knew why: for to
have her assent required to such a proposition,
at such a moment, was the strangest thing in
the world.

The vicar's ruddy countenance had grown
quite pale.

"If a man should come asking to marry
Emily, and his people concealed—necessary
facts from us—hoping she would be the saving
of him——"

Then there passed a dreadful moment of
silence in that glowing room, so bright with
sunshine. The three looked in each other's

faces—they were as if they had been struck dumb. ·

" Oh, Charles, Charles ! " said Mrs. Wynyard, and began to cry ; " Oh, *papa !* "

It was a name she still sometimes called him, in kindness, for the children's sakes.

" Father," said Emily, faltering, " in such cases people judge for themselves. They hate any one who interferes—— "

" As you would that men should do unto you, do you also unto them," the vicar replied.

" If it was my case," she cried, colouring high, " I should not believe a word ! "

" Oh, papa," repeated his wife, " papa ! you will not say anything ! Your own son, and perhaps the only hope."

" Father, if he was responsible for a woman's happiness—he has never had any responsibility : and if he loses her—as he says—— "

" And he always had the kindest heart ! " cried Mrs. Wynyard, among her tears.

" Get me the time-table," said the vicar ; " at least they must judge for themselves. I am going to town by the next train."

II.

THE vicar was asked into a handsome room in a hotel somewhere in Mayfair. He had got the address from Jack, who gave it with sus-picion and reluctance, not knowing what his father could mean, or what he wanted dashing up to town like this.

" Do you mean to tell me you're engaged to Miss Boldero ? " the vicar said.

" Why, yes ; of course we are engaged. Should I have written to the mater about it, do you think, if it hadn't been true ? But you never believe a word I say," Jack answered, with a certain defiance.

" I believe this, Jack, since you say it to

my face. Does this girl know anything about you?"

"This girl! You might be more civil to my betrothed. Of course she knows everything she has any call to know about me——"

"And she has a father?"

"She has a father," said Jack, beginning to feel there was trouble in the air.

"It is right that he and I should talk the matter over," said the vicar.

"If it's about money," said Jack, more and more alarmed, "they know I've got no money; there is no use entering upon that."

"There is use in entering upon—a great many things," the vicar said.

"Father, what do you mean? You are not going to—you don't mean to—spoil my chance!" cried the young man, "the only chance I ever may have in my life!"

The vicar said nothing. He gave his boy a look that silenced Jack. When had his

father spoiled a chance, or taken a hope away
from him? But there was nothing more to be
said to him now.

It was a handsome room for a room in a
hotel, being the best; and in the corner near
the great window which commanded a glimpse
of Piccadilly, there was seated a young lady
alone—a tall girl, with fair hair frizzed upon
her forehead, an unexceptionable toilette, and a
clear-cut imperious face. There is something
a little faulty, something peculiar, in the
American mouth. Heaven knows all our
mouths are faulty in all nations—it is the
peccant feature everywhere. In France they
say it of the English, whose long teeth are a
frequent subject of mockery : but the American
mouth has a character specially its own. It is a
little harsh, the merest trifle in the world under-
hanging—nay, too slight for any such decided
expression ; let us say with the under lip the
least in the world protruding beyond its fellow—

18

" Her lips were thin,
Except the one was next the chin."

But, on the other hand, that is too complimentary, for the underlip was as thin as the
other, only put forward a hair's breadth. It is
the result, I suppose, in the young feminine
subject of having things too much her own
way. She was looking at the vicar's card,
which he had sent up, when he entered the
room, and she said, with a little start, but
without rising—

" Mr. Wynyard, Leighton-Furness Vicarage.
Goodness! You are Jack's papa! "

" Yes, I am Jack's papa," said the vicar, half
astonished, half confused—half, nay, not half,
for three halves cannot be—but the very least
bit amused. He took the hand she held out to
him and held it for a moment. She looked a
creature who might do this thing—imperious,
not hesitating or counting the cost, whatever
she might take into her head.

" And you also have a papa," said the vicar.

" Yes ; I suppose Jack has told you all about us—how we met him, and how we did this bold thing and came after him here ? "

" He did not say you had come after him. I should have been very angry if he had."

" Why ? it is quite true. I liked him—I don't feel the least ashamed—better than any man I have seen ; and I thought, perhaps, it was the money kept him back. You are so ridiculously poor in this country. Why are you so poor ? So we came after him, papa and I—— "

" Was papa aware of—of what I may call the object of the journey ? " said the vicar, not knowing whether to laugh out, which, perhaps, she would not have liked, or what to do.

" Oh," said this young lady, " I never hide anything from papa."

" He is not in, I fear," said the vicar.

" Yes, he is in ; do you want him ? Tell me

first before I let you see him what are you
going to tell him about Jack?"

"My dear young lady, the two fathers must
certainly be permitted to talk such a matter
over."

"No," said the girl, "unless you tell me first
what you are going to tell him about Jack."

"I am going to speak to him very seriously,"
said the vicar. "It is a very serious thing to
confide the happiness of a girl like you to a
young man you scarcely know."

"Oh!" she said, "that's taking it the wrong
way about—confiding his happiness to me, you
mean. Oh, I am not at all afraid; I'll make
him happy. You need not make yourself
miserable about that."

The vicar pressed his hat—a hat which had
a rosette, as somebody has said, a sort of daisy
in it, for he was a rural dean, whatever that
may be—between his hands. The girl's eyes
were fixed upon that little symbol of ecclesi-

astical rank. She interrupted him before he could say any more.

" What is that for?—that thing in your hat? You are perfectly delightful for a papa-in-law. You make me more and more satisfied that I came."

" My dear," said the vicar, feeling that his virtue was stealing away from him under these blandishments, " I must see your father."

" Why?" she said. "I am sure I will do better. It is I that am to marry Jack, and not father. I'll hear what you have got to say."

" I called on Mr. Boldero," he said, more and more anxiously ; " permit me to ring and ask if he is in the hotel."

" Oh, he is in the next room," she said, " but he would not come in, of course, when he heard I was talking to somebody. Father!" she said, raising her voice.

A door opened, and a tall man put in his head. "Do you want me, Childie?" he said.

"I don't want you; but here is a gentleman who wants you. It is Mr. Wynyard, papa; Jack's father."

"I am happy to make your acquaintance, sir," said Mr. Boldero.

Both father and daughter spoke with an accent which was extremely piquant to the vicar. He had scarcely ever encountered any of their country-folk before, and he was extremely curious about them, and would, had his mind been less deeply engaged, have been greatly amused and delighted with their unaccustomed ways. Mr. Boldero was clad very solemnly in black, and doubtless had other peculiarities besides his accent; but the vicar was not at sufficient ease to remark them.

"I heard only this morning," he said, "of the engagement—if it is an engagement—between your daughter and my son Jack: and I came up to town instantly to see you."

" If it is an engagement ! " said Miss Boldero
with indignation.

" Well, sir, and have you any objection ? "
said the other father.

" Will you grant me an interview, Mr.
Boldero ? "

" With pleasure ; isn't this an interview ?
Fire away," said Miss Boldero's papa.

The vicar did not know what to say. He
sat still for a moment with the spirit gone out
of him. Then he murmured almost with a
supplicating tone, " I meant a private interview,
Mr. Boldero."

" Oh," said the American, " I have no secrets
from my Childie here. She's full of sense, and
always gives me her advice. Besides, if it is
anything about Jack, it is she that has the best
right to hear."

The poor vicar stared blankly in the face of
this man, who, being a man and his own con-
temporary, ought surely to have understood

him. He had thought that no man could have been more surprised than he had been this morning by the news of Jack's engagement. But he was more surprised now.

"My dear sir," he said, "it is impossible that I can say what I have to say in the presence of Miss Boldero——"

"Oh, never mind me," said the young lady. "He has come to tell you something against Jack, papa. I ought to be here——"

"It will be more fair," said Mr. Boldero.

"It is just simply indispensable," said his daughter.

The vicar felt the obstinacy of despair come into his being. He said—

"This is a very serious matter; I must talk to you alone. For Heaven's sake grant me ten minutes when your child's happiness is at stake. It is not all such easy work, such plain sailing as you seem to think."

"Father," said Miss Boldero, "if he tells you

Jack has another wife living or anything of that sort, promise me you'll not believe him."

She raised herself slowly from her seat.

" No, I'll not believe him without proof."

" I shan't, with volumes of proof. But I'll go away, though I consider it very uncivil and just like an Englishman to treat a woman in this contemptuous way. You said ten minutes, Mr. Wynyard. I'll come back in ten minutes to hear what all this fuss is about."

The young lady retired accordingly. She had a fine, graceful figure, and moved languidly, swinging a little to one side and another as some tall people do; and she went no further than to the next room, where it would not have been difficult to hear all that passed. But one could not see that young person and suspect her of listening at a door.

" Well," said Mr. Boldero, " out with it now. Is there another wife living ? I'll have to see all the papers before I'll believe that of Jack."

"Another wife!" cried the vicar. "God bless my soul, what can you be thinking of? Jack is not a villain!"

"Then there is not another wife? Well, that's a relief. What was a man to think? You're so dreadfully in earnest. If it ain't that, it's all right."

"But it is not all right," said the vicar. "Mr. Boldero, do you know my son has not a penny?—that is, there will be a mere trifle when we are both dead, his mother and I; but she's young yet, thank God. Stop a moment! And he is only a clerk in my friend Bullock's office, earning little, and, it breaks my heart to say, deserving little."

"An idle young dog; more fond of pleasure than of work. One can see as much as that, having, as you may say, the pleasure of his acquaintance, with half an eye."

"And there is more behind," said the vicar, very pale. "Don't make me blame my own boy more than I can help. God knows what it costs me to speak, but I can't let—the happiness of another young creature—be thrown away."

"Meaning Childie," said Mr. Boldero. "She's pretty well able to look after that herself. Hullo! you're not feeling faint, are you? Stop a moment; I've got something handy here."

"Never mind," said the vicar, waving him away. "Never mind; I'm all right. Mr. Boldero, do you understand what I say? Can I say anything stronger to make you understand? I dare not let you trust your daughter's happiness to Jack without telling you—— "

"Here, old man, take this, and sit down and keep quiet till you come to yourself."

And to tell the truth a mist was coming over the vicar's eyes. He laid his head back, and the room seemed to be gyrating round him. His heart was beating loud in his ears, and the tall figure standing before him with a glass in its hand seemed some kind of solemn demon tempting him to an unknown fate. He swallowed what was given to him, however, and slowly came to himself — the walls sinking into the perpendicular, and the tall American in his black coat becoming recognizable once more.

" You want to know, now, I suppose," said the other father, " how the young folks are to live ? I'm pretty comfortably off, and she's all I have in the world."

" Are you sure you understand me ? Do you know what I mean ? " said the vicar in despair.

" I know what you say fast enough; but what you mean is beyond me : unless it be to put a spoke in your son's wheel : which is more than I can understand, I'll allow."

The vicar did not say a word. They would think it at home, too, that he had tried to put a spoke in his son's wheel; and Jack would think it with more reason. But he felt that he had not another word to say.

"Have you got anything more to tell me in this hole-and-corner way?" the other father asked.

The vicar shook his head. "What does it matter what I have to say, when you won't believe me?" he said.

"Then I reckon I may as well have her back. Here, Childie," said Mr. Boldero.

And the door opened widely, and the young lady sailed in. "Well, papa," she said.

"Well, Childie. This old gentleman wants us to understand that his son is a bad lot, earns no money to speak of, and deserves less; is just good for nothing as far as I can make him out, not fit to be trusted with your happiness, he says."

"Father," said Miss Boldero, "who is talking of trusting Jack with my happiness? Is it the woman that asks the man to make her happy, or the man that asks the woman?"

"As a matter of fact it's the man; but I don't know that it always holds good. I must allow there is a doubt on that."

"There is no doubt in my mind," said the young lady. "Jack's happiness is going to be trusted to me, and I'll take care of it. If Mr. Wynyard has any objection to me he has got a right to say it."

"I ain't quite so clear of that," said Mr. Boldero. "Jack's of age; he's a man, and he has a right to choose for himself. The old gentleman has no call to have any voice in it."

Now, the vicar had gone on for a long time hearing himself called the "old gentleman," and had borne it; though at sixty, when a man is well and strong, it is an appellation which he feels to be half ludicrous and half injurious. But at last the moment had come when he could bear no more.

"The old gentleman," he said, "as you call me, has no desire to have a veto on his son's choice. You are a very pretty young lady, and charming, I am sure. But I don't know what are your other qualities, Miss Boldero. You must excuse me if I go now, for I have said everything I have to say."

"Go!" cried the girl, "without even having your luncheon!—you, who are going to be my papa-in-law?"

"Or a drink," said her father. "Yes, I had to give him a drink, or he would have fainted on my hands. Sir—if I must not call you an old gentleman—I'm a great one for knowing motives. What was your meaning in coming here to-day?"

"His meaning, of course, was to make acquaintance with me, papa, and see what sort of girl I was."

"Childie, let alone with your talk for one short moment, and let him speak."

The vicar stood up, and would have gone away if he could ; but the tall, black figure opposite barred the way, and demanded an answer. And, indeed, the answer was hard to give ; for a man somehow finds it very hard to say that he has done anything, whatever it may be, simply from the highest motive of all. The vicar felt this deeply, though he was an old gentleman, and though to be religious was, as you may say, his profession. He was often not at all abashed to avow a mean motive ; but when you think of it, it requires a great deal of courage to claim to be carrying out the charge of the Gospel. When he spoke his voice faltered, and his ruddy old face was like a rose. " Sir," he replied, adopting, without knowing it, the style of his questioner, " I have been preaching all my life what my Master said, ' Whatsoever you would that men should do unto you, do ye also unto them.' "

There was a little pause in the room, and

though the rattle of the carriages in the streets, and the sound of the men with the flowers calling, " All a-blowing and a-growing," came in very distinctly, yet the effect was as if you could have heard a pin fall. The boldest held his breath for a time—that is to say, even Miss Boldero, though she was not quite clear what it was all about, did not say a word. At last—

" That gentleman's Jack's father, Childie," said Mr. Boldero slowly. " I'm not in the running with the likes of him. If you don't train that fellow up to do his father credit, I'll never believe in you again."

" I will, papa," said the girl, as if she were making a vow.

*   *   *   *   *

Jack Wynyard strolled in in the afternoon, very carefully dressed, with a flower in his coat, but with much trouble in his mind. Why did his father come up to town so suddenly ? What was it he was so anxious to say ? The

19

young man's conscience told him pretty clearly
what it was, and he went to the hotel to fulfil

"JACK."

his engagement with his betrothed, expecting
little but to be met by her father, and sent

about his business, as the result of what his own father had said.

But no such reception awaited him. He found Miss Boldero in her prettiest toilette waiting for him. "And oh, Jack," said that young lady, "there has been the sweetest old gentleman here with a button in his hat, saying all sorts of things about you. He said you were not fit to be trusted with my happiness, and I said no; but I was to be trusted with yours. And we are going down to the vicarage to stay; do you hear, to stay, and make acquaintance with everything. And papa has fallen fathoms deep in love with him. And you are to behave, sir, like a saint or an angel, or I will lose all my credit with everybody from this day."

The vicar went home, I need not say, with a load lifted from his heart. He had delivered his soul, and yet he had not injured Jack. But that was because the people whom he had warned, in the discharge of his bounden duty, were such people as never were.

"They know everything at least," he said to his wife and Emily, who met him with much anxiety at the gate, both of them looking ten years older. "I have not concealed anything from them. But how it will all end God knows."

GENERAL PASSAVANT'S WILL.

By GRANT ALLEN.

I.

WE three girls had always been brought up to
expect we would come into Grandpapa Passavant's money. But there!—poor dear grandpapa, though he was the very sweetest old man
that ever lived, was stuck as full of prejudices
all over as a porcupine is stuck full of quills.
He literally bristled with them. He was always
flaring up at some unexpected point. And
what was worse, his family had, almost every
one of them, managed to annoy him by running
counter to his pet hobbies, for no better reason
on earth than just because they wanted to

marry the men or women they loved themselves, instead of marrying the people poor

GENERAL PASSAVANT.

grandpapa in his wisdom would have chosen to
select for them. It was really a most unfor-

tunate affair all round: one would say a
Passavant couldn't manage to fall in love with
anybody anywhere without treading on one
of poor dear grandpapa's very tenderest
corns.

There was Aunt Emily—for example—*she*
married an Austrian hussar; a very nice man
to be sure, and a Graf or something, at that;
but, somehow, dear grandpapa never could
abide him. He was military to the core, was
grandpapa, with a fine old crusted British dislike of "Frenchmen"—which was his brief
description for foreigners in general: a pretty
thing, he used to say, this marrying of people
in an enemy's service! Why, any day a
European war might happen to break out,
in which case we might be compelled to
take sides against Austria (though it doesn't
look likely, I must confess); and then, where
would Emily be? Why, we should all be
fighting against our own brothers-in-law and

sons-in-law! Preposterous! Absurd! "Depend upon it, Ethel, my dear," he used to say to me, stroking my front hair with his gentle old hand—for he was a dear old man, mind you, in spite of his prejudices—"depend upon it, Ethel, an Englishwoman's business is to marry an Englishman—a fine, strapping young fellow—and make him happy. What husband can you see among all those outlandish, jabbering, undersized foreigners to equal a British soldier—an officer and a gentleman?" For poor grandpapa's ideas never travelled one inch outside the Army List. That any girl of his could care to marry a curate, for example, or a barrister, or an artist, or a doctor, was a notion that never even so much as occurred to his dear old military head as for one moment possible.

Then there was Aunt Charlotte: *she* married a Scotchman. That was a harder blow still to poor grandpapa; for he hated the Scotch, and

he hated the Welsh, and he hated lawyers, and
he hated Presbyterians; and Aunt Charlotte's
husband was a member of the General
Assembly, and a Writer to the Signet. Grandpapa never quite grasped what the Signet was,
or why any one should write to it, but he always
alluded to Mr. Greig's profession with bitter
contempt. There are no such things as Writers
to the Signet in England, I believe; and
grandpapa considered everything un-English
as too barbarous and low for his mind to dwell
upon.

But poor dear Aunt Louisa had the worst
luck of all. *She* married a Portuguese Jew,
who was a member of the Stock Exchange.
That cut poor grandpapa to the very quick;
for Mr. Da Costa wasn't undersized at all: he
was six feet two, and as handsome as a
sculptor's model. Grandpapa never could bear
even to mention Aunt Louisa's name to us;
though he was very kind and good to her, and

to Mr. Da Costa, too ; and, when he died, he left her ten thousand pounds—the same sum he left to his other daughters—" as a slight token," he said in his will, " of Christian forgiveness." 'Twas a very hard wrench, but poor grandpapa bore it with manful resignation. He was accustomed to wrenches, he said, for one arm was amputated.

My father, however, who was a Colonel of Engineers, rejoiced the General's heart by marrying, as he ought, an Englishwoman, and a member of the Church of England. And though dear grandpapa never quite forgave us for being girls instead of boys, he was very proud and fond of us, and loved to contrast us (very much to our advantage) with those flat-faced little Germans, and that raw-boned young Malcolm Greig—for he never so much as deigned to allude in any way to poor little curly-headed Montague Da Costa.

So when, in course of time, dear grandpapa

died, and his will was opened, we were not at all
surprised to find he left a comparatively small
sum to papa, and twenty thousand pounds
apiece to his beloved grand-daughters, Linda,
Maud, and Ethel.

But there was a condition attached—a condition so awfully like dear grandpapa! " Provided always," the will went on in each case,
" my said grand-daughter abstains from marrying any of the three persons following—to wit,
firstly, an alien, whether naturalized or otherwise ; that is to say, any man who is not a
natural-born subject of Her Majesty Queen
Victoria : *secondly*, a Presbyterian ; that is to
say, a member of the Established Church of
Scotland : or, *thirdly*, a sworn broker of the
City of London. And in case my said grand-
daughter Linda," for example, " should break
this stipulation, and marry any of the persons
so excepted, then and in that case I will and
devise that she shall forfeit all claim to the

said sum of twenty thousand pounds, Consolidated Three per Cent. Annuities, standing in the name of my said trustees, which sum shall thereafter be divided into two equal moieties of ten thousand pounds each, whereof my executors shall pay over one moiety to my grand-daughter Maud, and the other moiety to my grand-daughter Ethel, for their own sole use and benefit."

II.

PAPA read the will over to us a few days after poor grandpapa's funeral, and explained what it meant in plain English, for of course we girls couldn't understand just at first all the legal technicalities. However, we knew, at any rate, we were now heiresses in a small way; and papa put it clearly to us that, as we had no mother (I forgot to say she died when I was five years old), we must be very careful, on our own account, not to let ourselves get entangled in foolish engagements with interested fortune-hunters. We must avoid young men who made themselves agreeable to us. But above all, he insisted—since poor grandpapa had willed it so—we must take particular notice not to fall in love, whatever might happen, with foreigners, Presbyterians, or members of the Stock Exchange.

That was easy enough to promise, I thought, for (being grandpapa's grand-daughter, you see) I hate Germans, I detest the Scotch, and I simply and solely abominate City men. So I made up my mind that, whatever the others did, I at least would keep a good hold over my own twenty thousand, letting Linda and Maud, in their various romantic ways, behave as they might with their separate portions.

Half an hour after papa had finished explaining the position to us, however, I was sitting in my own room, making day-dreams after my fashion, when suddenly there came a nervous little knock at the door, and, to my great surprise, enter Linda, excited. I could see at a glance the poor girl was very much flurried about something, for her face was pale, and her eyes were red; besides which, she instantly turned the key in the door in a most resolute way, and flung herself upon the bed as if her heart was breaking. Though Linda was four years older than me, she always came to me in all her troubles.

"Oh! Ethel," she cried, between her sobs, "this is too, too dreadful. I've been leading him to suppose for months that . . . well, that, if anything was ever to happen to poor dear grandpapa, he and I could be married; and now—this hateful, hateful will! I can't bear it. I can't endure it. How can I ever tell him?"

I was utterly taken by surprise. I didn't know who she meant. I could hardly believe my ears. Linda engaged to somebody for months before, and me never to have observed it! Never even to have suspected who on earth she was speaking of! This was almost incredible.

"*Him!*" I exclaimed, bewildered. "Why, who's he, Linda? I haven't the remotest notion who it is you're talking about."

Linda raised her head, open-mouthed, and gazed across at me, half-incredulous. "You don't mean to say, dear," she cried, with a sort of spasm of surprise, "you've never even noticed it!"

"Never, dearest," I answered sincerely, holding her hand and smoothing it. "Who is it? Mr. Mackinnon?" For he was really the only Scotchman of our acquaintance I could remember at the moment as at all a likely person for Linda to fall in love with.

"Mr. Mackinnon!" Linda repeated, half-angrily. "Mr. Mackinnon—indeed! Well, really, Ethel, I do think you might give me credit for better taste than that! No, it isn't Mr. Mackinnon. I wouldn't for worlds say a word about it to Maud—she'd be so unkind and unfeeling: she never cared for him; but I can trust *you*, dear, I'm sure: you're always so sympathetic, and I just *must* tell somebody. Well, for eight months past—I wonder you never guessed it—I've been engaged quite quietly to Charlie Vanrenen. Only, on poor grandpapa's account, both Charlie and I thought it was better for the present to say nothing about it."

Before I could answer there came a knock at the door again, and I heard Maud's voice saying, in a very cold, despairing way, " Ethel, let me in, please: I want to speak at once with you!"

Linda started up with a perfectly tragic air. "Oh, send her away, dear!" she cried, in a low, tremulous tone. "If *she* were to find out what I was saying, I could never, never, never marry poor Charlie!"

"You can't come in just now, Maud," I answered, going over to the door; and, speaking through the keyhole, "I'm—I'm writing letters." But that was a fib—I hope and trust a harmless one. "Come back again in half an hour, there's a dear, and I'll accept your confidences."

And I went over to the bed once more and tried my best to soothe down Linda. "Why, what's the matter," I asked, leaning over her and wiping her eyes, "with poor Mr. Vanrenen? He isn't a German, and he isn't a Dutchman; he isn't a Presbyterian, and he isn't a stockbroker. Why on earth should poor grandpapa's will interfere with you in any way? I understood Mr. Vanrenen was some sort of a writing person—a journalist, don't they call it? And poor grandpapa, though his prejudices were sufficiently comprehensive,

20

never made any express stipulation against the literature of our country."

But Linda began to cry again, even more bitterly than before. " Yes, Charlie's a news-paper man," she said, through her tears; " he's on the European edition of the New York *Tribune :* and he's been brought up in England; and he's as English in every way as you or I are ; and he only earns about three hundred a year, and he couldn't marry on *that*. But, Ethel, the dreadful thing of it all is this—he's an American citizen, and he's never been naturalized ! "

I pursed my lips. It was clear at once this was a hopeless case. There was nothing for it but to comfort her and condole with her. And I comforted her with all the consolation in my power. As far as *I* was concerned, I said, *my* share in her twenty thousand pounds—— But at that poor Linda grew absolutely hysterical. It was with difficulty I quieted her down by

"MAUD SEATED HERSELF WITH GREAT DIGNITY IN THE EASY CHAIR, FOLDED HER HANDS IN FRONT OF HER, AND STARED AT ME FIXEDLY."

degrees, and got her off at last to her own room to write a ten-page letter on the subject to " Charlie."

III.

THE moment she was gone, Maud, who had evidently been listening at her own door to hear mine open and let Linda out, came sweeping in, like a duchess in distress, pale and calm, but profoundly miserable. She seated herself with great dignity in the easy-chair, folded her hands in front of her like a marble statue, and stared at me fixedly for several minutes in solemn silence.

" Well, this is a dreadful thing," she said at last, with an evident effort, " about poor grandpapa's will ! I'm sure I don't know how on earth, after this crushing blow, I shall ever have the courage to face him and tell him ! "

" Tell who ?   Tell him what ? " I exclaimed, bewildered once more; for I certainly never suspected such a cold creature as Maud of being in love with anybody.

Maud gazed back at me with the tranquillity of utter despair. " Don't pretend you don't know, Ethel," she cried, in a very frigid voice. " It isn't any use.   You *must* have noticed it."

" Not Mr. Vanrenen ! " I cried, perhaps just a trifle mischievously.

The curl of Maud's lip would have been a study for Sarah Bernhardt.   " Well, really, Ethel," she said, bridling up, " at a moment like *this* you might at least spare me from positive insult !   Mr. Vanrenen, indeed !   That affected idiot !   I should be very hard up for a lover, I'm sure, if I allowed Mr. Vanrenen to presume upon proposing to me. . . . But you surely must know !   You can't possibly have overlooked it !   There's only one man on earth I'd ever dream of accepting. . . . I wouldn't tell Linda for worlds—Linda's so sympathetic. But you're always kind. I don't mind confessing it in this crisis to you—for it *is* a crisis. . . . I've been engaged for six weeks past to Malcolm Mackinnon."

" But he can join the Church of England," I said, coolly ; for I'm afraid I must confess, being a worldly creature, 1 didn't think the difference worth losing a wife for.

" No, no, my dear, he can't," Maud answered, with an air of resignation. " That's just the worst of it. His father's something or other in the high legal way to the General Assembly —Assessor, or what-not—and Malcolm's agent for the legal business in London. If he were to give up the Kirk, he'd lose his place, and his father might too, for it would be quite a scandal in Edinburgh. And he's only a junior partner, and he's too poor to marry. But I'll wait for him for ever, Ethel, grandpapa or no grandpapa; and I'll marry him when I choose. And I'll give up everything on earth for him; and you and Linda are welcome to your money, I'm sure; for I mean to marry Malcolm if he hasn't a ha'penny!"

I couldn't have believed it of Maud. But I rushed up to her and kissed her.

She sat there for half an hour, as cold as ice, and then went off in turn to write the news to "Malcolm." And as soon as she was gone I sat down and cried a little by myself for both of them. But, I must confess, I reflected with pride that the whole episode did the family credit. I was glad the two girls should have made up their mind to marry poor men, when they might have gone in, if they wished, for position or money; and I made up my mind at the same time that I, at least, would avoid the very first approach of aliens, Presbyterians, and members of the Stock Exchange. It's so very much easier not to fall in love at first

than, having fallen in love once, to fall out
again comfortably.

IV.

For the next few weeks life was a burden to
me. I lived in a perpetual state of receiving
alternate confidences from Linda and Maud, and
endeavouring to conceal from each the other's
position. This was distinctly hard, but I
pulled it through somehow. And I applauded
each in turn in her firm resolution that, come
what might, she would never give up her
Charlie or her Malcolm.

Fortunately, I myself was *not* engaged.
Forewarned was forearmed. I was in a
position, I thought, to give a wide berth now
to all classes of men expressly included in poor
grandpapa's interdict.

However, it was only about six weeks later

that I met at the Markwells' a most charming young man, who really paid me a great deal of attention. I liked him from the very first, though I pretended I didn't. His name was Kirkwood, and he was ˏa struggling artist. Now, artists had always for me a certain romantic interest; and, do you know, it may be silly of me, but somehow I never could bear to marry a man unless he were struggling. I can't say why; but well-to-do men always *did* repel me—they put my back up. I hate their smug, self-satisfied air, and I love the actuality, so to speak, of the struggling classes. Men who work for their living are always more real to me. Besides, Mr. Kirkwood was so retiring and unassuming; and I knew why. He liked me very much—I could see plainly from the very first; but he'd heard that I was an heiress, and he didn't want to marry me, because I had money. That's the only kind of man I should ever care myself to marry;

and I won't deny to you—in confidence—I thought a great deal, for the next ten days or so, in the solitude of my own room, about that delightful Mr. Kirkwood.

A stockbroker, indeed! With five thousand a year! Fancy marrying a stockbroker, in a world where there are men who can paint such beautiful things as he did—and live on next to nothing! It would be simply ridiculous.

Still, I wasn't going to be taken by surprise. I wouldn't allow myself, even, to begin falling in love the tiniest little bit in the world with that charming painter—at least, I thought not —before I'd satisfied myself thoroughly that he was a natural-born subject of her Majesty the Queen, and a member of the Church of England as by law established. Both those points I satisfactorily got out of him in the course of conversation; and then I made up my mind that, come what would, papa or no papa, if Mr. Kirkwood asked me—why, I wouldn't think it necessary to say " No " outright to him.

One afternoon, some weeks later, to my great delight, Mr. Kirkwood asked us all three to go round to his studio, with Mrs. Markwell and Bella to do the proprieties for us. Well, Linda refused ; but Maud and I went, and he showed us his pictures—oh, such lovely pictures! though I'm sorry to say he hardly ever sold them. And Mrs. Markwell was *so* kind ; she stopped behind in one room with the other two girls, while he took me into another behind it, to show me the piece he was then at work upon.

I don't remember much about that piece, I admit, though it was really lovely, for he talked to me a great deal about other subjects —mostly our two selves, I fancy—yet not at all as if he were making love to me. He spoke rather regretfully, as if he liked me very much, but could never ask me. And I knew very

"'THESE ARE CLEVER,' I SAID, LOOKING AT HIS SKETCHES."

well why. I saw it in his face. It was that horrid money that stood between us.

How I wished I was penniless—if Mr. Kirkwood preferred it so !

At last he took down a portfolio of sketches from a cabinet in the corner, and showed them to me by the window. They were earlier sketches than any I had yet seen of his—done evidently before he had taken to art as a regular profession. " These are clever," I said, looking at them with my head on one side, and pretending to be critical; " but they haven't such a sense of *technique*, I fancy, as the ones in the studio." I thought " sense of *technique*" was decidedly good, and, like a girl that I was, I wanted to impress him with my knowledge of things artistic.

" Well, no," he said, smiling, and looking hard into my eyes ; " those are early attempts. They were done, don't you know, when I was still on the Stock Exchange."

I gave a sudden start. "On the Stock Exchange!" I cried, puzzled, and just a wee bit tremulous. "You don't mean to tell me, Mr. Kirkwood, you were ever on the Stock Exchange?"

"Oh yes, I was," he answered, in the most matter-of-fact tone on earth. "But I did no good at it, you know; I'm not cut out for business. I was always daubing or making thumb-nail sketches when I ought to have been watching the rise and fall of stocks. So I left it at last as a bad job, and took to painting instead, which is my natural *métier*; though, of course, I'm still theoretically and legally a sworn broker of the City of London."

I turned so pale at those words that he looked at me in surprise. "That's very awkward!" I cried, taken aback, and trembling violently. Then I grew fiery red, for I saw in a moment I'd put my foot in it.

"Why awkward?" he asked, coming closer

and looking hard in my face. "You're faint, Miss Passavant! You're trembling! Let me run and get you a glass of water."

"Not for worlds," I cried, stammering and trying to recover myself. "I only meant——"

He seized my hand, and held it tight. He guessed the truth, I think. At any rate, he quivered. "You must tell me!" he cried. "Oh! Miss Passavant, what is it?"

"By my grandfather's will," I began; then I stopped and faltered.

He let my hand drop short. "Oh yes, I forgot," he said, in a disappointed tone; "I should have remembered that before; I shouldn't have dared to approach you."

I saw what he meant in a second, and I felt I really *must* tell him now. "But by my grandfather's will," I gasped out, in an agony of shame, remorse, and terror—for I felt it was horribly unwomanly of me to have let him see like that into my very heart—"we were to forfeit it all if we—oh! Mr. Kirkwood, I can't say it—if we any of us married an alien, a Presbyterian—or a sworn broker."

Before I knew where I was, something strange had happened. He was holding me in his arms, and pressing me tight to his breast. He was covering me with kisses. "Ethel—my Ethel!" he cried; "then it's all right, after all! You'll have no money! And you'll never mind! I know you'll be mine! What's money to you and me? With *you* to help me, I'm sure I can earn enough for both of us. It was only that horrid, horrid shadow that stood between us!"

I knew he was right, so I stood still and allowed him.

Two minutes later Mrs. Markwell came in upon us. I suppose I looked horribly flushed and flurried; but I understood I was engaged to Arthur Kirkwood.

V.

NEXT day I made a clean breast of it all to
Maud. She listened in silence, in that calm,
cold way of hers; then she took my hand in
hers, and, to my immense surprise, kissed me
most affectionately. " Ethel," she said, with
a burst, " I always knew you were a brick! I
knew you'd follow the guidance of your own
heart. But Linda's so different. *She'll* never
fall in love, you may be sure, with any one on
earth who could possibly come under poor
grandpapa's prohibitions. She's absolutely
mercenary!"

In the astonishment of the moment I blurted
out the whole truth. " Why, Maud," I exclaimed, " you're awfully unjust to her! She's
in love already—and with an American, too—
an alien—a foreigner—well, there, Mr. Vanrenen."

It was a shocking breach of confidence, I admit; and the moment I'd let the words pass my lips I regretted it bitterly. But Maud drew back like one stung; then she jumped up with a sudden air of resolve. "If that's so," she said quickly, in quite a hopeful tone, "I must see Malcolm immediately. Malcolm will tell us; he's so clever, Malcolm is. I see a way out, I think. But you're quite sure of this thing about Linda, are you, Ethel?"

"As certain as I am about you and Mr. Mackinnon, Maud," I replied, all bewildered. "Though I don't see what difference that can possibly make to you and me, dear."

Instead of answering, Maud looked at me hard once more, in her calmly contemptuous way— Maud had always a very low opinion of my humble intellect. Then she rose at once, and swept out of the room, with her train behind her, leaving me in utter wonder as to what on earth she could be driving at.

That very afternoon, as soon as lunch was finished, Maud asked Linda and myself to go out for a stroll in Kensington Gardens. From the way she asked it, we saw at once she had something definite in view; and, though Linda was the eldest, when Maud asked us in her grand manner to go anywhere, or do anything, we other two girls would as soon have dreamt of refusing to obey her as of refusing to obey a judge in ermine. So we followed her blindly through Palace Gardens, and past the Round Pond, and along the path to the seat under the trees by the Speke Memorial.

As we reached the seat, somebody got up and raised his hat to greet us. He was expecting us, clearly. I saw at a glance it was Mr. Mackinnon.

Maud took his hand in hers without a gleam of recognition, yet I could see he held it a *little* bit longer than was absolutely necessary. "You got my note, then?" she said, in her commanding voice. "And you've looked this matter up for us, Malcolm?"

"Yes, Maud," Mr. Mackinnon answered, just a trifle confused, and glancing askance from her to me and Linda.

"Oh, never mind the girls," Maud said, quietly, with a little wave of her hand. "They're all in the same box, you see. They won't turn back upon us. Tell us quite plainly what the law is in the matter."

"Well, I've consulted the will," Mr. Mackinnon replied, drawing an envelope from his pocket; "and I've consulted the authorities, and the result is, I find, that if your sister Linda marries Mr. Vanrenen——"

"Oh, Ethel, how could you!" Linda cried, turning towards me one red flush, and drawing back several paces in a tragic attitude.

But Mr. Mackinnon took no notice of her. "And if your sister Ethel marries Mr. Kirkwood," he went on; "and if, finally, you marry me, why, then, according to your grandfather's will, which the Courts would certainly uphold in every particular, your sister Linda's share must be divided equally between you and Ethel; your sister Ethel's share must be divided equally between you and Linda; and your share must be divided equally between the other two. So, you see, it cancels out. Each of you'll get just the same in the end, and all will come square, as if there were no restriction."

"Malcolm," Maud said, emphatically, moving back a step and surveying him from head to foot with supreme satisfaction, "I call you a Daniel come to judgment—yea, a Daniel! This is just delightful."

"And what's more," Mr. Mackinnon went on, looking from one of us to the other, "the arrangement would in every way be a most satisfactory one: for the original bequests are left under trust, and subject to many most vexatious restrictions ; while the reversions, by a singular oversight, are absolute, and for your own sole use and benefit."

" Girls," Maud said, triumphantly, " you hear him. This is capital. Do you agree to marry and make this redistribution ? "

" Certainly," I answered, without an instant's hesitation. " And so will you, Linda, as soon as you've had time to make out what it's all driving at."

I never saw a man more astonished in my life than poor dear papa when we explained to him the decision at which we'd all arrived. And I never saw a man more baffled either than Arthur Kirkwood when he found out that he'd have to take me after all, burdened with a fortune of twenty thousand pounds, which he'd never expected. It lost him such a chance of romantic poverty with the girl he loved that I really believe, if he hadn't been very much in love with me indeed, he'd have thrown me overboard at once, and started afresh in quest of a penniless damsel. But he managed to put up with it for my sake, he said, and you can see me as his Rosalind in this year's Academy.

APPLETONS' TOWN AND COUNTRY LIBRARY.

PUBLISHED SEMI-MONTHLY.

87. *Not All in Vain.* By ADA CAMBRIDGE.
88. *It Happened Yesterday.* By FREDERICK MARSHALL.
89. *My Guardian.* By ADA CAMBRIDGE.
90. *The Story of Philip Methuen.* By Mrs. J. H. NEEDELL.
91. *Amethyst:* The Story of a Beauty. By CHRISTABEL R. COLERIDGE.
92. *Don Braulio.* By JUAN VALERA. Translated by CLARA BELL.
93. *The Chronicles of Mr. Bill Williams.* By RICHARD M. JOHNSTON.
94. *A Queen of Curds and Cream.* By DOROTHEA GERARD.
95. *"La Bella" and Others.* By EGERTON CASTLE.
96. *"December Roses."* By Mrs. CAMPBELL-PRAE
97. *Jean de Kerdren.* By JEANNE SCHULTZ.
98. *Etelka's Vow.* By DOROTHEA GERARD.
99. *Cross Currents.* By MARY A. DICKENS.
100. *His Life's Magnet.* By THEODORA ELMSLIE.
101. *Passing the Love of Women.* By Mrs. J. H. NEEDELL.
102. *In Old St. Stephen's.* By JEANIE DRAKE.
103. *The Berkeleys and Their Neighbors.* By MOLLY ELLIOT SEAWELL.
104. *Mona Maclean, Medical Student.* By GRAHAM TRAVERS.
105. *Mrs. Bligh.* By RHODA BROUGHTON.
106. *A Stumble on the Threshold.* By JAMES PAYN.
107. *Hanging Moss.* By PAUL LINDAU.
108. *A Comedy of Elopement.* By CHRISTIAN REID.
109. *In the Suntime of her Youth.* By BEATRICE WHITBY.
110. *Stories in Black and White.* By THOMAS HARDY and Others.
110½. *An Englishman in Paris.* Notes and Recollections.
111. *Commander Mendoza.* By JUAN VALERA.
112. *Dr. Paull's Theory.* By Mrs. A. M. DIEHL.
113. *Children of Destiny.* By MOLLY ELLIOT SEAWELL.
114. *A Little Minx.* By ADA CAMBRIDGE.
115. *Capt'n Davy's Honeymoon.* By HALL CAINE.
116. *The Voice of a Flower.* By E. GERARD.
117. *Singularly Deluded.* By the author of Ideala.
118. *Suspected.* By LOUISA STRATENUS.
119. *Lucia, Hugh, and Another.* By Mrs. J. H. NEEDELL.
120. *The Tutor's Secret.* By VICTOR CHERBULIEZ.
121. *From the Five Rivers.* By Mrs. F. A. STEEL
122. *An Innocent Impostor, and Other Stories.* By MAXWELL GREY.
123. *Ideala.* By SARAH GRAND.

Each, 12mo. Paper, 50 cents ; cloth, 75 cents and $1.00.

New York: D. APPLETON & CO., Publishers, 1, 3, & 5 Bond Street.

BOOKS BY SARA JEANNETTE DUNCAN.

THE SIMPLE ADVENTURES OF A MEMSA-HIB. By SARA JEANNETTE DUNCAN. With 37 Illustrations by F. H. TOWNSEND. 12mo. Cloth, $1.50.

"It is impossible for Sara Jeannette Duncan to be otherwise than interesting. Whether it be a voyage around the world, or an American girl's experiences in London society, or the adventures pertaining to the establishment of a youthful couple in India, there is always an atmosphere, a quality, a charm peculiarly her own."—*Brooklyn Standard-Union.*

"It is like traveling without leaving one's armchair to read it. Miss Duncan has the descriptive and narrative gift in large measure, and she brings vividly before us the street scenes, the interiors, the bewilderingly queer natives, the gayeties of the English colony."—*Philadelphia Telegraph.*

"Another witty and delightful book."—*Philadelphia Times.*

A SOCIAL DEPARTURE: How Orthodocia and I Went Round the World by Ourselves. By SARA JEANNETTE DUNCAN. With 111 Illustrations by F. H. TOWNSEND. 12mo. Paper, 75 cents; cloth, $1.75.

"Widely read and praised on both sides of the Atlantic and Pacific, with scores of illustrations which fit the text exactly and show the mind of artist and writer in unison."—*New York Evening Post.*

"It is to be doubted whether another book can be found so thoroughly amusing from beginning to end."—*Boston Daily Advertiser.*

"For sparkling wit, irresistibly contagious fun, keen observation, absolutely poetic appreciation of natural beauty, and vivid descriptiveness, it has no recent rival."—Mrs. P. T. BARNUM's Letter to the *New York Tribune.*

"A brighter, merrier, more entirely charming book would be, indeed, difficult to find."—*St. Louis Republic.*

AN AMERICAN GIRL IN LONDON. By SARA JEANNETTE DUNCAN. With 80 Illustrations by F. H. TOWNSEND. 12mo. Paper, 75 cents; cloth, $1.50.

"One of the most naïve and entertaining books of the season."—*New York Observer.*

"The raciness and breeziness which made 'A Social Departure,' by the same author, last season, the best-read and most-talked-of book of travel for many a year, permeate the new book, and appear between the lines of every page."—*Brooklyn Standard-Union.*

"So sprightly a book as this, on life in London as observed by an American, has never before been written."—*Philadelphia Bulletin.*

"Overrunning with cleverness and good-will."—*New York Commercial Advertiser.*

"We shall not interfere with the reader's privilege to find out for herself what, after her presentation at court and narrow escape from Cupid's meshes in England, becomes of the American girl who is the gay theme of the book. Sure we are that no one who takes up the volume—which, by the way, is cunningly illustrated—will lay it down until his or her mind is at rest on this point."—*Toronto Mail.*

New York: D. APPLETON & CO., 1, 3, & 5 Bond Street.

MANY INVENTIONS. By RUDYARD KIPLING.

Containing fourteen stories, several of which are now published for the first time, and two poems. 12mo, 427 pages. Cloth, $1.50.

"The reader turns from its pages with the conviction that the author has no superior to-day in animated narrative and virility of style. He remains master of a power in which none of his contemporaries approach him—the ability to select out of countless details the few vital ones which create the finished picture. He knows how, with a phrase or a word, to make you see his characters as he sees them, to make you feel the full meaning of a dramatic situation."—*New York Tribune.*

"'Many Inventions' will confirm Mr. Kipling's reputation. . . . We would cite with pleasure sentences from almost every page, and extract incidents from almost every story. But to what end? Here is the completest book that Mr. Kipling has yet given us in workmanship, the weightiest and most humane in breadth of view."—*Pall Mall Gazette.*

"Mr. Kipling's powers as a story-teller are evidently not diminishing. We advise everybody to buy 'Many Inventions,' and to profit by some of the best entertainment that modern fiction has to offer."—*New York Sun.*

"'Many Inventions' will be welcomed wherever the English language is spoken. . . . Every one of the stories bears the imprint of a master who conjures up incident as if by magic, and who portrays character, scenery, and feeling with an ease which is only exceeded by the boldness of force."—*Boston Globe.*

"The book will get and hold the closest attention of the reader."—*American Bookseller.*

"Mr. Rudyard Kipling's place in the world of letters is unique. He sits quite aloof and alone, the incomparable and inimitable master of the exquisitely fine art of short-story writing. Mr. Robert Louis Stevenson has perhaps written several tales which match the run of Mr. Kipling's work, but the best of Mr. Kipling's tales are matchless, and his latest collection, 'Many Inventions,' contains several such."—*Philadelphia Press.*

"Of late essays in fiction the work of Kipling can be compared to only three—Blackmore's 'Lorna Doone,' Stevenson's marvelous sketch of Villon in the 'New Arabian Nights,' and Thomas Hardy's 'Tess of the D'Urbervilles.' . . . It is probably owing to this extreme care that 'Many Inventions' is undoubtedly Mr. Kipling's best book."—*Chicago Post.*

"Mr. Kipling's style is too well known to American readers to require introduction, but it can scarcely be amiss to say there is not a story in this collection that does not more than repay a perusal of them all."—*Baltimore American.*

"As a writer of short stories Rudyard Kipling is a genius. He has had imitators, but they have not been successful in dimming the luster of his achievements by contrast. . . . 'Many Inventions' is the title. And they are inventions—entirely original in incident, ingenious in plot, and startling by their boldness and force."—*Rochester Herald.*

"How clever he is! This must always be the first thought on reading such a collection of Kipling's stories. Here is art—art of the most consummate sort. Compared with this, the stories of our brightest young writers become commonplace."—*New York Evangelist.*

"Taking the group as a whole, it may be said that the execution is up to his best in the past, while two or three sketches surpass in rounded strength and vividness of imagination anything else he has done."—*Hartford Courant.*

"Fifteen more extraordinary sketches, without a tinge of sensationalism, it would be hard to find. . . . Every one has an individuality of its own which fascinates the reader."—*Boston Times.*

New York: D. APPLETON & CO., 1, 3, & 5 Bond Street.

THE FAITH DOCTOR. By EDWARD EGGLESTON, author of " The Hoosier Schoolmaster," " The Circuit Rider," etc. 12mo. Cloth, $1.50.

" One of *the* novels of the decade."—*Rochester Union and Advertiser.*

" The author of ' The Hoosier Schoolmaster' has enhanced his reputation by this beautiful and touching study of the character of a girl to love whom proved a liberal education to both of her admirers."—*London Athenæum.*

" ' The Faith Doctor ' is worth reading for its style, its wit, and its humor, and not less, we may add, for its pathos."—*London Spectator.*

" Much skill is shown by the author in making these ' fads' the basis of a novel of great interest. . . . One who tries to keep in the current of good novel-reading must certainly find time to read ' The Faith Doctor.' "—*Buffalo Commercial.*

" An excellent piece of work. . . . With each new novel the author of ' The Hoosier Schoolmaster' enlarges his audience and surprises old friends by reserve forces unsuspected. Sterling integrity of character and high moral motives illuminate Dr. Eggleston's fiction, and assure its place in the literature of America which is to stand as a worthy reflex of the best thoughts of this age."—*New York World.*

" It is extremely fortunate that the fine subject indicated in the title should have fallen into such competent hands."—*Pittsburg Chronicle-Telegraph.*

" This delightful story would alone be sufficient to place Dr. Eggleston in the front rank of American writers of fiction."—*Chicago Tribune.*

" The subject is treated with perfect fidelity and artistic truthfulness."—*The Critic.*

" LA BELLA " AND OTHERS. By EGERTON CAS-TLE, author of " Consequences." Paper, 50 cents ; cloth, $1.00.

" The stories will be welcomed with a sense of refreshing pungency by readers who have been cloyed by a too long succession of insipid sweetness and familiar incident."—*London Athenæum.*

" The author is gifted with a lively fancy, and the clever plots he has devised gain greatly in interest, thanks to the unfamiliar surroundings in which the action for the most part takes place."—*London Literary World.*

" Eight stories, all exhibiting notable originality in conception and mastery of art, the first two illustrating them best. They add a dramatic power that makes them masterpieces. Both belong to the period when fencing was most skillful, and illustrate its practice."—*Boston Globe.*

ELINE VERE. By LOUIS COUPERUS. Translated from the Dutch by J. T. GREIN. With an Introduction by EDMUND GOSSE. Holland Fiction Series. 12mo. Cloth, $1.00.

" Most careful in its details of description, most picturesque in its coloring."—*Boston Post.*

" A vivacious and skillful performance, giving an evidently faithful picture of society, and evincing the art of a true story-teller."—*Philadelphia Telegraph.*

" The *dénoûment* is tragical, thrilling, and picturesque."—*New York World.*

Recent Volumes of the International Scientific Series.

A **HISTORY OF CRUSTACEA.** By Rev. THOMAS R. R. STEBBING, M. A., author of "The Challenger Amphipoda," etc. With numerous Illustrations. 12mo. Cloth, $2.00.

"Mr. Stebbing's account of 'Recent Malacostraca' (soft-shelled animals) is practically complete, and is based upon the solid foundations of science. The astonishing development of knowledge in this branch of natural history is due to the extension of marine research, the perfecting of the microscope, and the general diffusion of information regarding what has been ascertained concerning the origin of species. . . . This volume is fully illustrated, and contains useful references to important authorities. It is an able and meritorious survey of recent crustacea."—*Philadelphia Ledger.*

"In all respects an admirable piece of work."—*The Churchman.*

"One of the most valuable and entertaining volumes in the series. . . . The author is master of an engaging style, and offers words of cheer and counsel to the beginner who may be dismayed by the bewildering riches of the crustacean world. Every branch of the subject treated is presented in the most interesting and significant light."—*London Saturday Review.*

H **ANDBOOK OF GREEK AND LATIN PALÆOGRAPHY.** By EDWARD MAUNDE THOMPSON, D. C. L., Principal Librarian of the British Museum. With numerous Illustrations. 12mo. Cloth, $2.00.

"Mr. Thompson, as principal librarian of the British Museum, has of course had very exceptional advantages for preparing his book. . . . Probably all teachers of the classics, as well as specialists in palæography, will find something of value in this systematic treatise upon a rather unusual and difficult study."—*Review of Reviews.*

"A well-arranged manual from the hands of a competent authority. . . . Of the nineteen chapters contained in the volume, seven deal with preliminary topics, as the history of the Greek and the Latin alphabets, writing materials, the forms of books, punctuation, measurement of lines, shorthand, abbreviations, and contractions; five are devoted to Greek palæography, seven to Latin."—*The Critic.*

"Covering as this volume does such a vast period of time, from the beginning of the alphabet and the ways of writing down to the seventeenth century, the wonder is how, within three hundred and thirty-three pages, so much that is of practical usefulness has been brought together."—*New York Times.*

M **AN AND THE GLACIAL PERIOD.** By G. FREDERICK WRIGHT, D. D., LL. D., author of "The Ice Age in North America," "Logic of Christian Evidences," etc. With numerous Illustrations. 12mo. Cloth, $1.75.

"The author is himself an independent student and thinker whose competence and authority are undisputed."—*New York Sun.*

"It may be described in a word as the best summary of scientific conclusions concerning the question of man's antiquity as affected by his known relations to geological time."—*Philadelphia Press.*

"The earlier chapters describing glacial action, and the traces of it in North America—especially the defining of its limits, such as the terminal moraine of the great movement itself—are of great interest and value. The maps and diagrams are of much assistance in enabling the reader to grasp the vast extent of the movement."—*London Spectator.*

www.ingramcontent.com/pod-product-compliance
Lightning Source LLC
Chambersburg PA
CBHW030916270326
41929CB00008B/720